The U.S. News Guide to Paying for College

From the editors of U.S. News & World Report

Published by U.S. News & World Report,
Washington, D.C.
Print ISBN: 9781629215686

Published by:
U.S. News & World Report is a multi-platform publisher of
news and analysis, which includes the digital-only U.S. News
Weekly magazine, www.usnews.com,
www.rankingsandreviews.com, and annual guidebooks on Best
Colleges, Best Graduate Schools, and Best Hospitals. Focusing on
Health, Money, Education, Travel, Cars, and Public
Service/Opinion, U.S. News has earned a reputation as the
leading provider of service news and information that improves
the quality of life of its readers. U.S. News & World Report's
signature franchise includes its News You Can Use® brand of
journalism and its "Best" series of consumer guides that include
rankings of colleges, graduate schools, hospitals, mutual funds,
health plans, and more.

Table of Co

Chapter 1: Should Parents Pay for College? 1
By JULIE MAYFIELD and LINDSEY MAYFIELD

Chapter 2: 12 College Financial Aid Terms Defined..5
By Scholarship America

Chapter 3: 5 Assumptions About College Aid..10
By KATY HOPKINS

Chapter 4: How College Savings Affect Financial Aid 20
By REYNA GOBEL

Chapter 5: Think Hard Before Borrowing For College 23
By EUGENE L. MEYER

Chapter 6: 6 Steps to Determine How Much to
Borrow for College 29
By KATY HOPKINS

Chapter 7: Smart Ways to Mix Student Loans and
College Savings...34
By REYNA GOBEL

Chapter 8: Save More for College Education With a 529 Plan 37
By NEDA JAFARZADEH

Chapter 9: Take These 4 Steps Before Opening a 529 Plan 40
By REYNA GOBEL

Chapter 10: 4 Reasons to Consider Purchasing
Another State's 529 Plan..43
By REYNA GOBEL

Chapter 11: Understand the Federal Tax benefits of 529 plans...................46
By REYNA GOBEL

Chapter 12: 5 Steps for Utilizing 529 College Savings
Plan Funds..50
By REYNA GOBEL

Chapter 13: Balance 529 Savings Plan Distributions with
Other College Funding 54
By REYNA GOBEL

Chapter 14: Review Your 529 Plan to Meet College
Savings Goals 57
By REYNA GOBEL

Chapter 15: Why A College Degree No Longer
Guarantees Success 60
By BROOKE BERGER

Chapter 16: College Majors with the best Return on Investment 64
By KELSEY SHEEHY

Chapter 17: Kick Off College Saving Before a Child is Born 71
By REYNA GOBEL

Chapter 18: Weigh Coverdell Accounts and IRAs for
College Savings Flexibility 75
By REYNA GOBEL

Chapter 19: 4 Overlooked Ways to Pay for College 79
By KATY HOPKINS

Chapter 20: How Parents Can Stretch College Savings
for Students Living at Home 84
By REYNA GOBEL

Chapter 21: 8 Ways to Save Money on College Textbooks 88
By Robert Berger

Chapter 22: 5 Big Financial Aid Lies 92
By KIM CLARK

Chapter 23: 4 Steps to Financially Prepare Your Student
for College 98
By KATY HOPKINS

Chapter 24: 4 Questions to Ask During Student Loan
Counseling 103
By KELSEY SHEEHY

Chapter 25: Parent Plus Loans: Frequently Asked Questions 108
By U.S. News Staff

Chapter 26: 6 Steps to Reducing Your Student Loan Costs........................111
By KIM CLARK

Chapter 27: Consider When to Use Private Student Loans 113
By KATY HOPKINS

Chapter 28: Consider These Options to Cut College Costs........................117
By JUSTIN SNIDER

Chapter 29: What Does Net Price Mean?...123
By KATY HOPKINS

Chapter 30: Why Prospective College Students Should
Be Using Net Price Calculators 126
By KATY HOPKINS

Chapter 31: 10 Things You Need To Know About
Net Price Calculators...129
By KATY HOPKINS

Chapter 32: How and Why To Get An On-Campus Job 134
By JULIE MAYFIELD, LINDSEY MAYFIELD

Chapter 33: 5 Financial Surprises for College Parents 137
By KATY HOPKINS

Chapter 34: How To Start Paying Off Student Loans 141
By KATY HOPKINS

Contributor Bios 145

Chapter 1

Should Parents Pay for College?

By JULIE MAYFIELD and LINDSEY MAYFIELD

In the world of higher education, some debates rage on and on: Public schools or private schools? Go Greek or stay independent? Should parents or children pay?

Given the dramatic increases in the cost of a college education, this last argument has taken on a new importance. Mother Julie Mayfield and her daughter Lindsey reflected on their experience with college payment.

JULIE:

My husband and I were on the same page early on about college educations for our kids. We would pay for them, if at all possible. Still, we know and respect families who have made a different decision. If your family is working that out now, here are some considerations to keep in mind.

1. What is your retirement situation? The choice to pay for a child's education is certainly a personal one, but most financial

experts agree on one point: parents should not sacrifice their retirement funding in order to pay for their kids' educations.

The reasoning is simple: while there are a number of ways to pay for college (loans, work, community colleges, and more), no one is going to give you a loan for your retirement. That is entirely on you. So, much like putting your own oxygen mask on before helping your child, get your retirement funding figured out before writing checks for higher education.

2. Does your child have a stake in his or her education? All children are different, but most will appreciate their educations more when they're required to play a financial role. Even though we foot much of the funding for Lindsey's college costs, she is still required to keep her GPA high enough to keep her scholarships. She also works part time to cover her spending money. While she has always been a self-motivated student, these two things keep her aware of the investment that's being made in her education.

Of course, for some families, parents footing the bill for a student is not a possibility. My husband was one of those students, and it's probably no accident that he has a strong work ethic. Even if you can pay for all of your child's costs, it's probably worth asking yourself if it's a good idea.

LINDSEY:

In high school, my parents made it clear that my main responsibility would be my schoolwork, before work or other activities. I always worked during the summer, but my "job" during the school year was simply to get good grades to secure good scholarship money.

I did that, and now that I'm in college, my grades are just as important. At the same time, however, I am older, more mature, and better able to juggle many responsibilities. Whether your parents are covering all of your college costs or you're expected to chip in, here are some of goals to set when it comes to funding my college education.

1. Grades always come first. When looking for jobs after college, work experience and GPA are both important. But to me, focusing on my studies is much more important than a part-time job to cover my personal spending money. (The one possible exception is if that part-time work is career-focused.)

I am lucky in that my parents are financially able to cover most of my college costs. If at all possible, parents should try to spare students the burden of working on top of a full course load, especially during the first year. Students who work may learn how to handle more responsibility, but they can miss out on things like participating in campus organizations, finding career-focused opportunities, and experiencing college traditions.

2. Budget even if you're not paying. One thing every college student should learn is how to keep a budget. Students who are not responsible for any of their own expenses (gas, food, clothes, social events, and more) may never learn how to control their own spending.

Too many of my friends have no idea how to track their spending when it comes to things like shopping, dining out, road trips, and the like. Even if parents are footing the bill, teaching students to recognize exactly where their money is going can be a real eye opener.

Chapter 2

12 College Financial Aid Terms Defined

By Scholarship America

Navigating the college financial aid process can be daunting even for the most highly educated among us. What are the differences among grants, scholarships, and loans? What does FAFSA stand for and who should complete it? And how does work-study actually work?

Your college education is an extremely important—and often extremely expensive—investment. Before you shell out thousands of dollars for an advanced education, give yourself a basic education of postsecondary financial aid. To help, we've put together a quick reference guide on common—and often confusing—financial aid terms. From award letters to tuition reimbursement, we've got you covered.

Award letter: Arriving in your mailbox around mid- to late April, your award letter basically outlines your financial aid package from the college(s) to which you applied. But be careful: Colleges aren't required to follow a standard format for award letters, and crucial information is sometimes missing or misleading—such as the cost of attendance! Colleges sometimes vastly underestimate the cost of transportation and textbooks, or make the financial aid package look more generous than it actually is.

Expected Family Contribution (EFC): This is the measure of your family's financial strength, and how much of your college costs it should plan to cover. This is calculated based on a specific formula, which considers taxed and untaxed income, assets, and benefits, as well as the size of your family and the number of family members attending college during the year. Your expected family contribution is calculated based on your FAFSA results.

FAFSA (Free Application for Federal Student Aid): You've probably heard of the FAFSA, but do you know what it is and just how important it can be for you and your family? Filling out the FAFSA is one of the first steps in the financial aid process, and determines the amount that you or your family will be contributing to your postsecondary education. The results of the FAFSA determine student grants, work-study, and loan amounts. We recommend that everyone fills out the FAFSA; it only takes about an hour to complete, and you may be surprised with the results.

Federal student aid: The largest form of student aid in the country, federal aid programs come in the form of government grants, loans, and work-study assistance and are available to students at eligible postsecondary institutions (colleges, vocational schools, and graduate schools).

Financial need: This is the amount of a student's total cost of attendance that isn't covered by the expected family contribution or outside grants and scholarships. A student must demonstrate financial need to be eligible for need-based financial assistance programs.

Grants: Did someone say free money? Unlike loans, grants—which can come from the state or federal government, from the college itself, or from private sources—provide money for college that doesn't have to be paid back. We'll take this opportunity here to remind you again to fill out the FAFSA; many grants determine eligibility by looking at your FAFSA results.

Loans: If scholarships and grants don't cover the entire cost of your tuition, you may have to take out a student loan to make up the difference. Federal student loans don't have to be paid while you're in college, and there are also a variety of loan forgiveness programs out there post-graduation. The rates and terms are generally more flexible than private loans.

Room and board: Everyone needs to sleep and eat. If you plan to do it on campus, those fees are part of your total cost of attendance.

Scholarships: There really isn't much difference between a scholarship and a grant, though the general consensus is that scholarships are primarily awarded for academic merit (good grades) or for something you have accomplished (volunteer work or a specific project); however, there are many need-based scholarships out there, as well. Like grants, scholarships don't have to be repaid.

Tuition: College tuition is the "sticker price" of your education, and does not include room and board, textbooks, or other fees. Colleges often calculate tuition based on the cost of one credit, or "unit." For example, a college may charge $350 per credit for an undergraduate class. Many times colleges will simplify this by providing a flat fee for tuition; you're often required to take a minimum amount of credits and cannot exceed a maximum amount of credits. "True cost" is a little misleading, since there are other costs on top of tuition.

Tuition reimbursement: Tuition reimbursement, also sometimes called "tuition assistance," is increasing in popularity. Some employers will refund you the cost of your tuition if you're studying a work-related area. Tuition reimbursement can cover as little as one or two courses, or can cover up to the entire cost of your education.

Work-study/work award: The Federal Work Study program provides funds to eligible students (see FAFSA above) for part-time employment to help finance the costs of postsecondary education. In most cases, the school or employer has to pay up to 50 percent of the student's wages, with the federal government covering the rest. You could be employed by the college itself; or by a federal, state, or local public agency; a private nonprofit organization; or a private for-profit organization.

Chapter 3
5 Assumptions About College Aid

By KATY HOPKINS

When it comes to deciphering college costs, there are warnings at every stage of the decision-making process: Don't rule out a college based on sticker price; be wary of comparing net price calculator outputs; and understand that not all student loans are created equal. Each disparity places much of the onus on future college students and their parents to thoroughly read and research in order to make well-informed decisions.

Even when an accepted student receives financial aid award packages from colleges, the necessary sleuthing isn't complete.

"I think every college thinks they are providing adequate information ... But when you're in the position of the parent and trying to track that information for multiple schools, it's all presented in completely different ways under completely different names," says Jane Kulow, a future college parent who blogs about her family's college decision process. "It takes, truly, a lot of detective work."

As you research and weigh your college options, avoid making these five assumptions:

Assumption 1: All components of your packages are free money. Financial packages might include two distinct categories of aid: money you won't have to do anything for, and money you will. It may sound like a simple premise, but it's important to realize what is essentially a gift—scholarships or grant aid—and what you'll have to work for or pay back: work-study positions and loans.

Early research into financial aid options helped Laura Turpin to differentiate the components of each of her daughter's three aid award packages. "Luckily, I've read enough ... to know what to look for [and] knowing the difference between what you don't have to pay back and what you do have to pay back, and then the differences between the different loans, ... different interest rates, stuff like that," she says. With her grip on various kinds of aid, she's since mapped out each of her daughter's offers in a categorized spreadsheet to help them keep track.

Assumption 2: Your awards will be renewable. Once you've discerned what is scholarship or grant aid, realize that those totals may fluctuate in subsequent years.

"If you've been offered a merit award from one particular institution, you'll want to find out: Is that merit award renewable? Do I need to maintain a high grade point average?"

notes Linda Parker, director of financial aid at Union College in Schenectady, N.Y.

Need-based aid, including Pell grants, are typically subject to congressional budget negotiations each year and are also not guaranteed for a student's entire time in college.

Assumption 3: The total you see is what you'll actually pay. "One piece of advice I got was to dig deeply into each college's website for all of the fees and the add-on things that they don't typically include in tuition and room and board," says future college parent Kulow. Understand that your financial aid award package might not include an accurate final estimate once additional costs such as travel and books are factored in.

Assumption 4: The total cost will hold steady until graduation. Unless you're attending a school with a tuition guarantee, there's a good chance that your college costs will be higher each year.

That's muddying the college decision for Turpin and her daughter, who has been accepted to both public and private schools. With budgets on the brink in many states, Turpin is wondering how drastically the costs at their public options may change.

"I think it's more of a crapshoot as far as how much their tuition will rise," she says. "I think all state schools have that issue."

Assumption 5: You can't negotiate. If you're very displeased with the financial aid package from your top-choice school, it usually doesn't hurt to contact admissions officers. If there have been any drastic changes to your family's financial situation, for instance, or if you've received a much better offer, it's worth trying to appeal.

At the least, calling a school's admissions office can serve as another step in your fact-finding mission before deciding where your high schooler enrolls in college. "Spend the time and dig deeply," Kulow recommends, "if [cost] is going to be an important factor in the student's decision."

You've drawn up a list of public and private colleges that are a good fit based on everything from academics to ambiance. The price tags vary widely, but don't automatically cross colleges off the list if they seem too expensive. Just because some schools are pricey doesn't mean you can't afford them.

Most institutions determine their financial aid packages depending on the size of their endowment, a family's financial need, and how much the school wants a particular student. Financial aid can become so generous, in some cases, that the most expensive private school may end up being cheaper to attend than a state university.

Yet how these institutions determine their awards packages can seem mystifying. The same student can apply to colleges with similar tuition rates and yet receive award letters that differ by thousands of dollars. Families "just don't know where to start," says Manuel Fabriquer, president of College Planning ABC, a San Jose, Calif.-based consulting firm. "They don't really understand what happens on the back end."

Basically, colleges all want to attract as many top-notch students as possible, but they have only so much money to go around. Each institution uses its own criteria to determine a family's financial need and adjusts the proportion of grants versus loans in the package depending on how desirable the student is.

According to the nonprofit College Board, the yearly average for tuition and fees for in-state students at public institutions is $8,244. That's an increase of about 42 percent since 2006, while the average annual tuition at private schools has increased 28 percent over the same period. So, even an extra $1,000 in grant money can go a long way. By educating themselves, families can navigate the system effectively and obtain the best possible financial packages.

When offering financial aid, many college and university officials claim to meet a student's "full need." This means that the total package offered to prospective students—which can be a combination of grants, federal and private loans, and work-study money—will fill the gap between the family contribution and the cost.

But exactly how need is determined, and how much schools will offer in grant money versus loans, is based on several factors. To start, most secondary institutions rely on one of two tools to help determine the "expected family contribution," or EFC.

Anyone applying for federal student aid will need to submit the Free Application for Federal Student Aid, or FAFSA, which asks detailed questions about family income, investments, savings, and other financial matters. The FAFSA form includes questions based on the family's tax returns for the previous year.

The second tool, the College Scholarship Service (CSS) Profile, created by the College Board, is more detailed. It's used widely, primarily by private colleges. The form asks about income and liabilities, including family assets, veterans benefits, and child support payments.

The application also includes a blank form for applicants to provide "explanations and special circumstances," such as a family's high medical bills or unemployment issues. Schools utilize the data to compute the EFC for each prospective student. They then take this baseline information and, using their own internal criteria, weight different factors more than others.

For example, some universities might allow families to deduct the cost of K-12 private school tuition, while others pay greater attention to the "special circumstances" section. All this, of course, means offering more or higher "merit" grants to desirable applicants, such as an accomplished pianist or a top lacrosse player.

Financial aid also helps different institutions gain an advantage over their rivals when trying to attract the most diverse, talented, and well-rounded students, says Sandy Baum, an independent policy analyst for the College Board and a senior fellow at George Washington University. On the flip side, students deemed less desirable are asked to foot more of their tuition bill from loans or work-study. "They just don't have enough dollars to go around, and somehow they have to ration it," Baum says.

As you prepare to make your case to colleges, experts suggest following these tips:

1. Get your data in order: Read through the FAFSA and CSS Profile fine print and ask questions so you know what is required when filling out the paperwork. For example, correctly identifying eligible income exemptions could mean a difference of tens of thousands of dollars in aid.

Consider the case of a couple who recently approached Fabriquer with $150,000 in loans from their son's schooling at Stanford University. The family income was only about $60,000 per year, but the small business owners had mistakenly listed their business assets on the FAFSA.

Business owners with fewer than 100 employees don't have to report such assets. It wasn't until after their son had graduated that they realized they would have qualified for need-based grants had they filled out the FAFSA properly. "They should have gotten a free ride," Fabriquer says.

2. Contact colleges early: Don't assume that the school knows about all the aberrations in your family's finances. Has a family member gotten sick, diminishing saving accounts? Did an inheritance inflate last year's income? Tell the college or university you've applied to, even before you've been accepted. The sooner schools know, the better.

3. Beat the deadlines: Don't wait until the last minute to contact the college or university and plead your case, says Rod Oto, associate dean of admissions and director of student financial services at Carleton College. Oto says his office gets as many as 20 calls or E-mails daily right before the May 1 decision deadline, overloading his four-person staff responsible for reviewing each applicant's situation.

"You're better off starting the conversation earlier, because it might not be just one conversation you're going to have," Oto says. Furthermore, there are limited funds available, so if you don't get in early, the money could be promised to someone else.

4. Understand the formula: Many universities include extraneous expenses in their cost of attendance calculations, but

they're not always easy to find. Tulane University, for example, is one school that does provide cost estimates for books, room, board, transportation, and miscellaneous items on its website. Do your homework to find out whether colleges have omitted or underestimated these extra costs.

5. Evaluate each piece: It's important to educate yourself on what is being given free and what you might be required to pay back later. Some grants may be provided for only one year, others for more. Also, check to see if merit scholarships are tied to maintaining a minimum GPA or a spot on a sports team. "Asking about what the aid package looks like in future years is important," says GW's Baum.

6. Be prepared to appeal: Brian Henson nabbed acceptance letters for fall 2011 from California Polytechnic State University—San Luis Obispo, the University of Texas—Austin, and the University of San Diego. But his father was laid off from his job in November 2010, dramatically affecting the family's income. Each school had offered Henson aid packages that were light on grants and heavy on loans. He honed in on Cal Poly, with a cost of attendance of about $22,000, and UT—Austin, with a price tag for out-of-staters at about $47,000.

A few weeks before the decision deadline, Brian's mother contacted both schools to plead for more grant money. "At first, with Texas it looked promising, as they said they could accommodate us and offer the whole amount" in grants, she says.

"But then they came back ... and said they couldn't because there wasn't any money left."

Brian ultimately chose Cal Poly. But had the Hensons contacted admissions officials at Texas sooner, they might have been able to obtain more grant money. Colleges often have funds to offer to students with extenuating circumstances like Brian's, whose dad is again employed.

7. Go right to the top: Not satisfied with the answers you're getting from an aid representative? Ask to speak with the director of financial aid. "Most of us are open to it and happy to talk to students and parents," Carleton's Oto says. Still, he adds, "Most financial aid offices are equipped to handle most requests. Whom you talk to doesn't matter as much as whether you have a strong case."

Chapter 4

How College Savings Affect Financial Aid

By REYNA GOBEL

Need-based financial aid awards for college don't just depend on a family's income. Students' eligibility for such aid could be decided in part by how much families have saved for their education, including in tax-advantaged 529 plan accounts.

That's because schools use a number called the expected family contribution, or EFC, to determine how much a family can afford to contribute to their child's education.

Varying formulas are employed based on whether a school uses a number calculated according to a legally established formula, with the income and asset information provided by the student and parents, on the Free Application for Federal Student Aid, or from data in the College Scholarship Service (CSS)/Financial
Aid Profile.

That figure is compared with the cost of attendance by schools to determine a student's eligibility for need-based aid.

Families generally get less aid as their expected family contribution comes closer to the cost of attendance.

Fred Amrein, a Pennsylvania-based personal financial adviser, says that in a family where the parents have a gross income of $160,000, their expected contribution – based on a number of factors such as the state they live in – is $39,500.

Generally, need-based financial aid can only be awarded up to the cost of attendance. In this example, if a child plans on going to a school where the cost of attendance is $30,000, the amount of savings wouldn't matter because the family's expected contribution based on income alone is higher than the cost to attend that school, he says.

However, if the student plans on going to a private school with an annual cost of attendance of $50,000, the family's assets will matter, he says.

Take a different example. If a family's income is not enough to meet the expected cost of attendance but the parents had a lot saved for college, those savings would be a greater factor in their expected contribution.

Age matters, too. Parents' 529 plan accounts and other savings count toward the EFC on a weighted scale based on the oldest parent's age, says Amrein. The older parents are, the less these funds factor into the expected contribution.

If the parents in the first example are 48 years old and have $80,000 in countable assets, their $39,500 expected contribution would increase by $2,100. Countable assets generally are taxable assets with the exceptions of home equity, small businesses and 529 plans. Retirement accounts do not count, Amrein says.

Keep in mind that a student's income and savings play a role in the calculation as well. If the student earns less than the standard tax deduction – $6,100 in 2013 – that income would not be expected to be a part of the family's contribution to the cost of college.

If that student had $10,000 in a savings account under his or her own name, about $2,000 would be added to the expected family contribution – nearly the same amount added by the parents' $80,000 in assets. Therefore, this family would have been better off saving for college in a 529 plan or savings account under a parent's name, Amrein says.

To plan ahead, students and parents can use the FAFSA4caster tool offered by the Department of Education. This tool gives parents the opportunity to plug in different variables such as asset levels and income to see how their expected contribution changes.

Chapter 5

Think Hard Before Borrowing For College

By EUGENE L. MEYER

Amanda Nazario turned down what she describes as a "phenomenal package" of financial aid at Syracuse University— only minimal federal loans involved—to attend George Washington University in the nation's capital. She graduated in May without regrets, but with $37,000 in debt and no idea how she'll pay it off.

Like many of her peers, Nazario, a native New Yorker who would like to go to law school and become a sports attorney, is just now gaining a concrete idea of how the rising cost of college has affected her. A recent College Board report puts today's tuition and fees for public four-year schools at more than 3.5 times the level of 1981, after adjusting for inflation. And costs at private four-year colleges are almost three times what they were 30 years ago.

The most recent widespread tally reveals that 2009 graduates of four-year colleges who had borrowed had an average debt of $24,000, according to the Institute for College Access and

Success (TICAS), a nonprofit research and advocacy group; other estimates put the 2011 load at more than $27,000. Students at some institutions take on much more: Last year, borrowers who graduated from Holy Names University in Oakland, Calif., owed an average of $48,800.

The amount of borrowing worries many experts; more than a few suggest that college-bound students in need of big loans seriously consider less costly schools. "There has to be some kind of reality check," says Mary Malgoire, a Bethesda, Md., financial adviser. Parents, she says, need to ask themselves, "'What are our resources? What will that get us? How much should be a burden on our children, on our own retirement?' Sometimes you have to ramp down expectations. We're no longer in an economy where the sky's the limit."

Rather than automatically accept all the student loans to which they're entitled, and perhaps also borrow privately to cover part of the family contribution, "I encourage students to borrow the minimum they need and live like a student in school, so you don't have to live like a student after graduation," says Mark Kantrowitz, publisher of Fastweb.com and FinAid.org, free websites providing comprehensive information about financial aid.

He thinks attending an in-state public university is one of the best ways to save on college costs; if you're serious about learning, you can expect "a very good return on your investment."

Research released in February by economists Alan Krueger at Princeton University and Stacy Dale of Mathematica Policy Research reaffirmed their finding of a decade ago suggesting that eventual earning power depends pretty much entirely on student qualities—talent, drive, ambition, and confidence, for example— rather than on the prestige of the chosen college.

A 2010 FinAid analysis of government data on student aid, moreover, shows that those graduating debt free are 70 percent more likely than people with loans to go on to graduate school. Granted, it's a balancing act. "Modest federal student loans can help you go to college full time without dropping out and limit your work hours so you have time to study and sleep," says Lauren Asher, president of TICAS.

A good rule of thumb, in Kantrowitz's view, is to limit your total debt to no more than your expected starting salary. By the end of October, U.S. colleges will be required to post a "net price calculator" on their websites to allow prospective students to see an estimate of the true amount they'll owe and will have to borrow.

Though financial aid budgets have been sorely strained in the tough economy, more than 70 schools have instituted no-loan policies for their low-income students—typically those with family incomes below $40,000 or $50,000. Half a dozen schools extend the policy to all students, and a number cap the amount offered in loans to higher-income families.

But "no loan doesn't necessarily mean no cost," Asher stresses. AtAppalachian State University in Boone, N.C., even families with incomes around $20,000 were expected to come up with $850 themselves in 2010-2011. At elite Amherst College in Massachusetts, the no-loan policy applies to all households, regardless of income. But expected contributions for dependent-student families who brought in between $90,000 and $120,000 a year were about $17,000 of the $54,000 sticker price in 2010-2011.

Parsing the college financial aid letter is key to calculating what the true load will be. It may seem obvious, but a loan doesn't lower your cost of college; with interest, it increases it. It's not always easy to tell from the aid letter which awards are grants and which are loans, so when in doubt, ask.

What are your borrowing options? Experts advise always seeking a government loan first because they are cheaper, the rates are fixed, and you have an option of different repayment plans. The government pays the interest on subsidized Stafford loans until graduation for families who qualify based on need. For dependent students, total borrowing is limited to $23,000 in subsidized loans and $31,000 in unsubsidized loans (minus what they receive in subsidized ones).

Interest rates on new subsidized loans awarded for this fall have fallen to 3.4 percent; the rate for unsubsidized loans is fixed at 6.8 percent. Parents can take out government PLUS loans up to the cost of tuition minus any student loans awarded. The rates are fixed at 7.9 percent, and there is a 4 percent fee. Private loans may offer currently competitive rates, but they're often variable, with no cap on rates or fees.

With federal loans, you might get a break on repayment, too. Several income-based repayment plans allow borrowers to make monthly payments based on their earnings and family size, and extend the term from the standard 10 years to 12 to 25 years. Graduates may also qualify to have their balances forgiven after 120 payments and 10 years of public service. But student loans are very difficult to extinguish by bankruptcy; wages, tax refunds, and even Social Security can be garnished to pay for them.

The experience of Lindsay McAfee, 29, a tax lawyer in Washington, D.C., who grew up in Des Moines, might be instructive. Though she had some help from her parents, she bore most of the cost of a bachelor's from George Washington University and a law degree from the University of Iowa, and is now paying off $165,000 in student loans at $1,100 a month. The payment is a "big burden, very, very painful," she says. She does not take lavish vacations. She does not own a car.

As her youngest sister was finishing high school this spring, McAfee passed along some of her insight. "I think you have to take a hard look at what you think you will earn with what you're studying," she told her sister. "I wouldn't trade my experience for anything, but I also would like not to have that debt." As luck would have it, McAfee's sister preferred Iowa State University.

Chapter 6

6 Steps to Determine How Much to Borrow for College

By KATY HOPKINS

Student loans are a popular way for students to cover some of the costs of college. But is borrowing for an education a good idea?

"Taking out a loan to pay for your education is an investment in yourself and your future," says Suzanna de Baca, vice president of wealth strategies at Ameriprise Financial. "At the highest level, it's a very positive use of debt. But like any debt, you do want to make sure you are not taking out an excessive amount, and that you will have the ability to repay it."

There's no one right number for all students to borrow, de Baca notes, but following these steps can help you arrive at a manageable amount:

1. Estimate your full cost of college: Figuring out what college will cost is not often a quick calculation—but it's a crucial step toward borrowing the correct amount of loan debt for you, de Baca advises.

"The first thing that any student needs to do is really, truly understand what the cost of their education is going to be," de Baca says. "People look at tuition and think, 'Oh, that's what I need.' They don't really make a good list of all the different expenses that are involved, and then match that with various ways to actually meet those needs."

When you're comparing financial aid packages from colleges, make sure you're factoring in costs including room, board, school materials, and transportation. Don't forget to factor in other means you'll use to cover costs, including grants and scholarships from schools, savings, and potential earnings from a part-time job.

2. Take only what you need: Student loans aren't free money. You'll pay back what you take and then some, after interest is accounted for—so make sure to be frugal when possible, de Baca recommends.

"Student loans are really intended for tuition, books, and room and board," she says. "The room and board is probably where there's some fungibility in terms of how a student might be thinking about their money. Students should try to keep their living and entertainment expenses as low as possible and not use those funds in inappropriate ways."

3. Research your earning potential: For a student loan burden to be manageable, the total amount you owe should be

less than your starting salary after graduation, notes Mark Kantrowitz, founder of FastWeb.comand FinAid.org.

"If your total student loan debt is less than your annual income, you'll be able to repay that debt in about 10 years," he says.

Forecasting your future at age 17 might seem hard, but researching the published salaries of recent graduates—both from colleges you're considering and majors you're interested in—can pay off down the road. To get started, explore online offerings such as NerdWallet's college comparison tool, which lists average starting salaries by major and college.

4. Think long term: It can be challenging to think about bills that won't come for years, but it's critical to consider the month-to-month implications of what you borrow. That's a commonly skipped step when it comes to taking a student loan, de Baca of Ameriprise Financial says.

Students can find repayment calculators online, including through financial aid sites FinAid.org and PayBackSmarter.com, that can help estimate monthly student loan payments. If you have a rough estimate of an average starting salary for your intended field, that's even better. Experts typically advise that monthly payments of roughly 10 percent of your income is manageable.

"It's always better for students and parents to be informed, and think about what the end will look like—not just what the first year looks like," notes Brian Lindeman, financial aid director at Macalester College in St. Paul, Minn.

5. Weigh loan options: Ultimately, your monthly payments may be affected by the type of loan you take.

Student loans fall into two main categories: federal and private. Federal loans, which are offered through the government, come with fixed rates and borrower protections, including the ability to lower or postpone payments if you experience financial hardship. Private loans may have fixed or variable rates and don't typically offer flexible student loan repayment options.

Even if you were to borrow the same amount, you could end up paying more for one loan than another, in interest or in missed opportunities to have. Make sure to thoroughly research your options to see which best fits your situation.

6. Keep a healthy mindset about debt: The horror stories of students drowning in hundreds of thousands of dollars of debt are, in reality, quite rare, financial aid expert Kantrowitz wrote in a recent paper, "Who Graduates College with Six-Figure Student Loan Debt?" Before you start to fret about student loans ruining your life, keep in mind that well-researched, manageable amounts of student debt can add a variety of positive aspects to

your educational experience, including motivation and real-life training, financial aid experts have noted.

"I think we've given the impression to some parents and students that borrowing at all is dangerous when it comes to college," says Lindeman of Macalester College. "So, it's a nuanced message that's difficult to deliver quickly and easily, but I think a reasonable amount of student debt can be one of the best investments a student will ever make."

Chapter 7

Smart Ways to Mix Student Loans and College Savings

By REYNA GOBEL

The 2008 plunge in stock values eroded Phillip Orzech's college savings.

The Connecticut parent's 529 plans, tax-advantaged investment accounts, were primarily comprised of stock-based investments. The accounts, which had held enough to pay for four-year educations for each of his two children, now only covered one year of tuition.

"We had less money saved than we thought there was going to be," he says. "We used what we had to pay everything that we could." He and his wife then borrowed student loans for their children to make up the difference.

For families who will use both student loans and 529 plan savings to pay for college, experts recommend the following.

1. Use available funds from other sources first: Families shouldn't take out student loans before considering payment plans, grants and scholarships.

Those who can afford to save some money from regular paychecks throughout the year can consider tuition payment plans. Also, students can contribute income from working part-time jobs during college.

"There is current income that can be used," says Charlie Rocha, senior vice president at Sallie Mae. "Most schools do have tuition payment plans."

Payment plan time frames vary but do give families at least a few extra months to pay tuition, Rocha says. Fees for payment plans are normally lower than student loan interest rates. If a family qualifies for an education tax credit, choosing a payment plan may allow parents to wait for a tax refund check, he says.

2. Don't pay back student loans with 529 plan funds: Paying back student loans with 529 plan contributions could be pricey.

"Student loan payments are not a qualified higher education expense," says Joan Marshall, executive director of the College Savings Plans of Maryland. "So if you borrow for college now, you cannot use funds saved in a 529 plan years later to pay student loans without also paying tax on any earnings, plus a 10 percent federal penalty on those earnings."

3. Pay close attention to cost of attendance: Every school lists the cost of attendance on its website. Student loans can be used to pay for any expense listed within the cost of attendance, but 529 plan withdrawals can only be used for what's known as qualified education expenses.

"Use 529 funds for college expenses while the student is in college, like tuition, room, board – if the student is attending at least half-time – and books before relying on student loans," Marshall says.

For example, the University of North Texas lists an average annual cost of attendance for the 2013-2014 school year as $19,324 for in-state residents. Tuition, fees, room and board and books and supplies account for $15,196 of that in-state total.

While families should try and pay as much as possible using sources other than loans, the $4,128 for transportation, personal expenses and federal student loan fees can't be paid with 529 plan funds without the possibility of paying a potential tax penalty. Families should try to pay for these costs with non-529 plan sources.

While it's hard to cover $15,000 every year without borrowing, families who saved for college reduce students' future student loan debt and payments.

"One of the main reasons families save for college in 529 plans is to reduce reliance on student loans, so now is the time to reap the benefits of those savings," Marshall says.

Chapter 8

Save More for College Education With a 529 Plan

By NEDA JAFARZADEH

When it comes to paying for your child's college education, do you feel prepared? Putting money aside in a regular savings account likely won't help you reach your goals the same way other savings vehicles can, like a 529 plan – an account specifically designed to encourage saving for educational costs.

Curious what a 529 plan is and how it works? A 529 plan is similar to a 401(k) plan, but whereas the latter type of account is used to build your nest egg, the former is used to pay for college expenses.

However, the tax advantages of a 529 plan are similar to a Roth investment retirement account since you pay federal income tax on your contributions, but then the earnings from your investments grow tax-free.

There are two types of 529 college savings plans: the prepaid plan and the savings plan.

529 college prepaid plan. With the 529 prepaid plan, you purchase tuition credits in your state's university system at current tuition rates. This means your child is protected against future hikes in tuition costs despite the likely increase in inflation. However, before opening a 529 prepaid plan, make sure your child plans to attend the school for which you are purchasing tuition credits to ensure the investment doesn't go to waste.

529 college savings plan. The 529 savings plan is a tax-advantaged account that allows you to accumulate assets that can be used toward any accredited college or vocational school in the United States. The funds can be used to pay for more than just tuition costs, including textbooks and other education-related fees.

Contribution limits. The annual maximum contribution allowed per person to either plan is $14,000, and if you are married, your spouse can contribute an additional $14,000 each year for a total of $28,000. Each spouse is also allowed to make a one-time contribution of $70,000 (five years worth of annual maximum contributions), but parents who opt for this will have to wait six years before they can start contributing again.

The total maximum contribution allowed on a 529 plan is $360,000 (market value) for each beneficiary. However, your assets can grow beyond that amount through investment gains.

Risk level and investment options. With a 529 savings plan, depending on the state, you can choose between several investment options based on factors such as your child's age, your asset allocation preference and investment risk level. You can also decide to invest your money in a portfolio of stocks, bonds and/or money market funds. However, don't assume your state's plan is the best option, as not all states offer tax deductions. If that's the case, you may want to open an account in another state with options that better suite your child's needs.

For a list of the best 529 plan options by state residency, see NerdWallet Investing's comparison of the top accounts.

Chapter 9
Take These 4 Steps Before Opening a 529 Plan

By REYNA GOBEL

Jeff Howkins remembers lying awake at night worrying about how he and his wife were going to send their children to college—before they had any.

Howkins, president of Sallie Mae's Upromise Investments, Inc., says he learned he didn't have to "eat the elephant in one bite." The Howkinses bought a $1,000 zero coupon bond, where interest accrues but is not paid out for years. By the time the Howkinses were ready to use it, the value of their investment grew to $15,000.

Howkins says buying the bond made him and his wife feel like he did something toward paying for college for their kids. "Parents worry about not saving enough and become discouraged," he says. But Howkins says saving for college doesn't involve writing and following a 20-page comprehensive report. Instead, he says, small actions create big results.

One such action might be to set up a 529 college savings plan. Follow these four steps to find time and money to start and fund a 529 plan:

1. Start a 529 plan piggy bank: Named for the section of the Internal Revenue Code under which they were created, 529 plans are college savings accounts that allow money to accumulate and be withdrawn tax free when used for education-related expenses. "Some 529 plans, such as the Utah Education Savings Plan, have no minimum dollar requirements," says Lynne Ward, UESP executive director. "Families can save as little or as much as they want." Parents who pay cash for all their purchases can save the change and, whenever their piggy bank fills up, deposit the money into their checking account so it can then be transferred into a 529 plan.

The same strategy can be applied to debit card purchases by rounding all debit card transactions to the nearest dollar each week and then transferring the difference into a 529. Saving $5 per week adds up to $260 per year. Over 10 years, parents or grandparents save $2,600 before any return on investments. If you earned a 4 percent return, you'd earn close to another $650.

2. Pick an uncomplicated 529 plan: If you're limited on time, try not to pick a plan with myriad investment choices. According to Ward, some plans have 20 to 40 investment options. Look for a 529 plan that has investment options that fit your needs.

"Age-based investment options are great for account owners who don't want to self-manage their account funds," says Ward.

3. Save systematically and within your budget: Setting an automatic monthly deposit into a 529 plan is an easy way for parents to remember to save, experts say. However, it's important to note that what savers can afford one month may not be feasible the next month. According to experts, parents should pick an amount they can afford in the month where their electric bill is at its highest, or when sales are the lowest if working on commission. Sending in extra cash when available is always an option.

4. Take advantage of free money from your state: "Check with your home state's plan first to see if any incentives are available," says Laura Lutton, author of Morningstar's "2011 529 College Savings Plans Research Paper and Industry Survey."

"Some states allow you to apply those tax benefits to any plan in the country, but often you lose your state's benefits if you go elsewhere." Based on information from her report, state benefits can total more than $1,000 in a year.

Chapter 10

4 Reasons to Consider Purchasing Another State's 529 Plan

By REYNA GOBEL

The state parents live in should not be the only reason for choosing a 529 plan, says Chadderdon O'Brien, financial planner at Lassus Wherley. Most 529 plans, investment plans designed specifically for college savings, are available to both in-state and out-of-state residents.

Plans vary in ability to switch 529s without tax penalty, minimum initial deposits, maximum contribution rules, and investment options and costs, as well as tax benefits, says O'Brien. Parents need to choose the 529 plan with the best combination of these features for them, regardless of the state of origin.

Here are four reasons for parents to consider choosing another state's plan:

1. Ability to move funds to another 529 plan without tax liability: Choosing a plan with the ability for parents to roll over

money from one 529 plan to another without state tax penalties can be important if there's a possibility that you'll move to another state or switch plans in the future, says Kristopher Johnson, senior financial advisor with Timothy Financial Counsel Inc.

For example, if parents who live in a state with a 5 percent income tax rate deposit $5,000 each into their state's 529 plan for 10 years, they'd save $5,000 in taxes. But if they move their money out of that state's plan, Johnson says, they could have to repay the tax savings plus a penalty.

In this case, he says it might be best to open a second 529 plan in the state the parents moved to in order to enjoy tax benefits in the new home state. The first plan will still continue to grow, and they wouldn't pay penalties.

2. Low minimum contribution: Parents who want to start contributing to a 529 plan but are short on funds may want to look around for plans with low initial deposits, also called a minimum contribution. According to O'Brien, most plans have low, reasonable minimums from $15-$25.

However, some plans start with even lower minimum deposits. For example, according to Utah Education Savings Plan Executive Director Lynne Ward, her plan has no minimum. Parents can start saving in the Utah Education Savings Plan by depositing a penny.

3. High contribution limits: The maximum contribution limit is the total amount you are allowed to deposit into one 529 plan. Most states' 529 plans have a maximum contribution range between $200,000 and $350,000.

While the amounts seem high, O'Brien says, "It's difficult to know what college expenses will look like in 10 to 15 years." Therefore, it's hard to know how much savings will be enough. Parents who have the means to deposit as much as necessary to pay for their child's future education should pay attention to maximum contribution limits when choosing a 529 plan.

4. No requirement to choose your state's plans to receive tax benefits: Some states do not have a state income tax. Other states have state income taxes and offer tax benefits for 529 plan contributions, but don't restrict which state's plan parents participate in while still claiming tax benefits. In these cases, Timothy Financial Counsel's Johnson says, plan price comparisons and investment flexibility become deciding factors.

For example, Nebraska's direct-sold 529 plan (a plan without a financial adviser) charges only 0.29 percent. Utah has slightly less investment fund flexibility, but charges just 0.15 percent to 0.20 percent in administrative fees, and investment options also have very low costs. Johnson says either of these plans are good options if tax benefits aren't a factor.

Chapter 11

Understand the Federal Tax benefits of 529 plans

By REYNA GOBEL

Mark Berg, a certified financial planner, knows he has two years of college savings for each of his three kids, partly because taxes aren't charged on withdrawals from their 529 plan accounts.

Unlike other investment accounts, earnings from savings account interest, bond interest, and stock and mutual fund value increases aren't taxed at time of sale or withdrawal, he notes. By saving within a 529 plan, families don't have to worry about paying taxes on withdrawals when their children start college.

Here's what every parent should do to maximize federal tax benefits.

1. Schedule regular contributions: If a couple with two children saved $100 monthly per child for 10 years, they would accumulate $24,000 before investment earnings. If the account grew in value by 5 percent per year, they would add another

$7,100 to their savings without paying taxes on the account's growth.

The exact tax savings would depend on whether the investments are in savings accounts and bonds or stocks and stock-based mutual funds, Berg says. Savings account and bond interest earned outside of 529 plans are taxed at the couple's income tax rate, while stock-market based investment growth would be taxed at the capital gains rate, a special tax rate for investment sales, he notes.

For example, a middle class family makes between $70,000 and $142,000 and withdraws half of the funds to pay for college in 2012. The investments are split between bonds and stock-based mutual funds. The taxes charged if the money was withdrawn this year is $1,400.

2. Combine federal tax benefits with state tax deductions: Many states offer income tax deductions for 529 plan contributions. For instance, Berg's home state of Illinois charges 5 percent income tax, but the state allows tax deductions for 529 plan contributions of up to $10,000 per individual tax payer, or $20,000 per couple.

A $10,000 contribution in a single year would save an Illinois resident $500 in taxes. If the same couple mentioned above contributed $2,400 this year, they would save $120 off their annual tax bill.

And if tax rates stay the same, this adds up to $1,200 of tax savings over a 10-year period. Combined with federal tax savings, that amounts to $2,600.

3. Don't limit investments during bad stock market years: Avoiding contributing to 529 plans when the stock market dips could prevent investment growth. Berg says he was able to average 5 percent annual growth because he bought stock-based mutual funds at low prices when his other stock-based mutual funds were falling in price during the 2008 financial crisis.

"There was no special trick to finding the funds, because generally stock prices fall in weak economies and rise again when the economy recovers," Berg says. But he cautions, "Reinvesting in stocks should only be done if you have time before your kids enter college."

His kids were 6, 9, and 10 in 2008. The total tax savings is based on when parents withdraw the funds to pay for their children's education, and not when they're earning it, he says. Continual investing averages out in long-term investment plans, Berg notes.

4. Before investing outside of 529 plans, consider what happens if taxes increase: "There is talk that capital gains could increase significantly, which would make 529 plans more

attractive since they grow tax free," says Fred Amrein, a Pennsylvania-based chartered financial consultant.

For example, a couple earned $5,000 in 10 years of investing in stock-based mutual funds within a 529 plan account.If taxes on earnings from stock-based investments rise from 15 percent to 20 percent, investing in a college savings plan saved $250 more than if the tax rate remains at 15 percent. Check with your financial adviser once per year about tax rates, Amrein says.

Chapter 12
5 Steps for Utilizing 529 College Savings Plan Funds

By REYNA GOBEL

Parents of students starting college this fall can finally withdraw the funds they've worked so hard to accumulate in their 529 plans, education savings plans with tax benefits.

But before parents request funds from their plan administrator or adviser, they have to be aware of key details, such as when tuition is due and how long it takes to ask for a distribution of funds and receive the check.

Parents should follow the following steps to withdraw funds from a 529 college savings plan:

1. Review the tuition payment due dates: Your first step in planning when to take distributions from a 529 plan is to look at the financial aid calendar on the university website, says HC Financial Advisors, Inc. Certified Financial Planner Karla McAvoy. "You don't want to be in a situation where, 'Oh my gosh, tuition is due Friday and it's Wednesday,'" she says. Start

the process of requesting funds at least five to 10 days before payment is required, McAvoy says.

2. Estimate time needed to cash out investments: The amount of time varies to withdraw money from a 529 plan because it's not as simple as calling the plan administrator or adviser to cut a check, says Certified Public Accountant and Personal Financial Specialist Jason Washo.

While some plans contain only money market or savings accounts, he notes most accounts contain mutual funds or short-term bonds. This means there has to be a settlement period for noncash investments to be sold or traded.

For example, Washo says, "a parent calls a plan administrator on Monday and tells them, 'I need $5,000.'" The plan administrator will place the trades, he says. "The funds won't be available till Thursday. The check is then cut Friday." By comparison, he notes, investments that are solely in savings or money markets are available the same or next day.

3. Consider potential delays: "If you deposit a $10,000 check and your average checking account balance is $2,000, your bank is probably not going to turn around and let you have access to that money the next day," Washo says. "If you deposit a check larger than your current balance, they bank is likely going to put a one-, two-, or maybe three-day hold."

Wiring money avoids check clearing delays, says McAvoy of HC Financial Advisors, Inc., but does require paperwork. Experts say it's a great option when tuition is due quickly or the extra fee is worth not waiting for the check to arrive in the mail. You'll still have to wait for noncash investments to sell or trade first.

4. Decide where tuition checks should be sent: While parents can request checks to be sent to the university or to themselves, Washo recommends that parents have 529 distribution money sent directly to them so they don't have to worry about confirming receipt of the checks by the university.

After the check from the 529 plan administrator clears their account, parents can pay tuition online and receive a receipt from the school website. If writing a check from a bank account, Washo suggests that parents send the check to their son or daughter so it can be hand delivered to the student accounting department.

5. Request distributions: Once parents complete their research of deadlines and time tables, it's time to request funds. Parents who enrolled in plans through an advisor should contact him or her when ready to withdraw funds, says Virginia 529 College Savings Plan spokesperson Scott Ridgely. Owners of direct 529 plans should contact the plan administrator for withdrawals.

No matter whether you request a check or have the money wired, save all receipts from the university and from the investment accounts, Washo recommends. Since 529 plans have a tax benefit, you might need to prove that 529 plan money was spent on education in the event of an audit.

Chapter 13

Balance 529 Savings Plan Distributions with Other College Funding

By REYNA GOBEL

It's tempting for parents to withdraw funds they've saved in a 529 plan, a higher education savings account with tax benefits, if their son's or daughter's freshman-year education costs are entirely paid for by scholarships, grants, and tax credits. But Ryan Law CFP®, director of the University of Missouri's Office for Financial Success, says it's not always a good idea.

Availability of funds can vary from year to year. In certain years, 529 plan distributions may be needed to supplement other forms of college funding, Law says. Other years, he notes, there may be enough funding without 529 plan funds.

Before parents withdraw their first dollar from 529 plans, they should follow these three steps:

1. Start with the cost of attendance: The cost of attendance, according to the Department of Education, is the total cost of going to school—from tuition to housing. This number is

available on university websites via cost of attendance calculators, such as this one from Louisiana Tech University. But parents can get a better estimate by discussing their son's or daughter's current or future college budgeting with someone in the student money management or financial aid office, Law says.

For instance, the university cost of attendance calculator doesn't track if particular majors require more lab fees or equipment charges, he says. Compare the revised college costs estimate with total grants, scholarships, and tax credits parents expect this year, Law says. Then supplement with 529 plan distributions as needed to make up the difference for qualified higher education expenses, education-related costs allowed to be paid with 529 distributions.

2. Consider factors affecting future availability of funding: Once you know if this year's college expenses are covered by grants, scholarships, grants, or tax credits, you can consider future years, Law says. He notes that availability of funding can change annually for a variety of reasons.

For example, scholarships that students receive one year may not be available the next. Four-year scholarships can even be rescinded; it's important for students and parents to know what can cause a student to lose continuation of a four year scholarship, Law says. For instance, Law was among 20 students who received a certain college scholarship during his undergraduate career. In order for his scholarship funds to renew, he had to maintain a certain GPA and complete a community service requirement.

Availability or amounts of federal grants and tax credits can also change at the discretion of Congress, Law says. In addition, changes in family income affect eligibility.

3. Avoid emptying 529 plans until education is complete: Parents aren't assessed a tax penalty on money withdrawn for a non-educational purpose equal to or less than the amount of scholarships or grants received within the same tax year, but they do have to pay income taxes on earnings, says Jason Washo, a personal financial specialist and certified public accountant.

The income tax paid is based on the parents' tax bracket, Washo says. For example, if a parent were to withdraw funds from a 529 account with $25,000 left in it—$12,500 was from money the parent contributed and $12,500 was from investment growth—at the end of a child's college career, he or she would be charged income tax on the half from earnings, Washo explains.

If the parent is in a 25 percent tax bracket—between $70,700 and $140,700 in income for 2012—the tax is slightly more than $3,000. If $10,000 of the $25,000 was withdrawn because of scholarships received in previous tax years, there would be an additional 10 percent penalty, equaling $500, on the portion from earnings. But the parent is still left with just under $21,400 that they can spend on anything they want, Washo notes.

Chapter 14

Review Your 529 Plan to Meet College Savings Goals

By REYNA GOBEL

Parents participating in a 529 plan, a college investment account with tax benefits, need to assess progress on meeting college savings needs on an annual basis, experts say. Investments may exceed or fall behind the growth that families were expecting, and the ability to make contributions may also change.

Two certified public accountants, Clare Levison and Michael Goodman, advise following these four steps to review your 529 plan's progress.

1. Define goals: "Parents should have clear goals of what they are able to provide in educational assistance," Levison says. The goal may be to pay for in-state schools or 50 percent of their child's education, she says. The amount of monthly contributions needed to fund this goal could change because of investment growth.

For instance, if parents are fortunate enough to see their investment value increase by $1,000 more than what they originally expected, transferring those funds from stock-based investments into a savings account—a safer choice—reduces contribution needs in the future. If the parents have five years left until their teen starts college, having $1,000 in guaranteed college funding reduces the amount needed in monthly contributions by around $17.

Parents calculating what they'll be able to pay for should also keep in mind potential increases to tuition over time, Levison notes.

2. Adjust contributions based on affordability: Since funding availability changes each year, it's important to define savings goals based on current finances, Levison says. Parents who start saving when their children are newborns won't earn the same annual income 18 years in a row.

They may earn raises and bonuses, but there may also be periods when they're unemployed or decide to put 529 plan contributions on hold until debt, such as from credit cards, is paid off, Levison says.

For instance, consider if a parent who's currently contributing $50 per month receives a pay increase of $200 per month after taxes, totaling $2,400 for the year. He or she may have also had a recent medical emergency that cost $1,000 and depleted emergency savings. After refilling the emergency savings account with $1,000, the parent would still have an extra $1,400 that year to deposit into a 529 plan.

Conversely, if the parent didn't receive a bump in pay, it's possible he or she might have had to reduce 529 plan contributions by $1,000 that year to make up the difference.

3. Adjust investments for safety: During your annual assessment for meeting goals, it's important to review investment choices and determine their safety.

If you saved better than you thought you would, you may want to move more of your investments to savings or money market accounts to protect a percentage of your investments, Levison says. "Safety of principal is sometimes more important than potential rate of return," she notes.

4. Adjust investments based on economic changes: Consider rebalancing investments based on market movements, advises Goodman, a personal financial specialist. For instance, in a weaker economy, parents may want to take some money out of safer investments such as savings accounts and money markets and gear investments more toward mutual funds, he notes. The goal is always to buy at low prices and sell at higher ones, Goodman says.

However, Levison adds that parents should carefully consider the percentage of funds moved away from savings. Everyone's risk tolerance is different, she says, and families should consult their local CPA, financial adviser, or 529 plan manager when considering significant plan changes.

Chapter 15

Why A College Degree No Longer Guarantees Success

By BROOKE BERGER

More Americans are going to college than ever before. Many graduates, however, are buried in debt with few job prospects. In "Is College Worth It? A Former United States Secretary of Education and a Liberal Arts Graduate Expose the Broken Promise of Higher Education" conservative pundit William Bennett weighs the relevance of a four-year degree against rising tuition costs. The Reagan administration official recently spoke with U.S. News about what prospective students should be thinking about, what they get for their buck and why a bachelor's degree is no longer synonymous with success. Excerpts:

Should Americans keep sending their kids to college?

Sometimes. But they shouldn't automatically or reflexively send their kids to college. They should pause and stop and think. It's not like deciding to have breakfast or go to bed. It's more like, say, to get married. It's a big decision. [There are] a lot of consequences, a lot of costs, a lot of ups and downs. Investigate it with your eyes open.

How does someone know if college is the right choice?

First, look internally. Why do you want to go? Is it just because everyone else is going? That's not a good enough reason. Is it because that's where the good parties are? That's not a good enough reason. To get away from the folks? That's not a good enough reason. What's your academic interest? How well does the school address that? What will you owe when you finish? What will your job prospects be?

What is different today about college than in years past?

First of all, a lot more people are going. But, oddly, a lot more of the public has questions about whether it's worthwhile to go. In 2008, 81 percent of adults thought college was a worthwhile investment. This year, 57 percent think so. The second thing, of course, is loan shock.

Why is college so expensive?

There are three main reasons. One is a lot of families, out of the goodness of their hearts and love of their children, will pay anything to send their kids to college. Two, many colleges will try to get as much money as they can. Three, the federal government endlessly subsidizes the increases in college and higher education. And so the price keeps getting higher. There's an academic arms race.

What are the most unnecessary costs at colleges and universities?

We have some great examples in the book, where if you look at places like High Point University, they're talking about things like climbing walls, gourmet restaurants, room service and hot tubs. If you're borrowing money, paying your own way, or maybe if you have a job, you can go to the Comfort Inn of dormitories. You don't have to go the Ritz-Carlton.

Can the situation be improved?

Yes, I do think there's a way this situation can be improved. One, we have to become aware of it. Sunlight is the best disinfectant. It's the 30th anniversary of "A Nation at Risk," that famous report about American high schools. We haven't had this conversation about colleges and universities. We need to have it. We hope this book initiates it in earnest.

What are students and their parents getting for their buck?

We actually point out in the book exactly what they're getting for their buck. We have charts on their return on investment, which will be, I think, a matter of some controversy where we use information gathered and put together by others. So, you can measure it in terms of actual dollars. The other thing I'd say is that when we talked to managers and employers, only 16 percent said the people they hire are ready for the workforce.

Is a four-year degree needed to succeed?

No. There's a statistic we cite in the book that by the year 2018 there will be 14 million jobs available, well-paying jobs, which will require more than a high school diploma but less than a college diploma. Right now, a graduate of a community college, which is a two-year college, on average, makes more than a graduate of a four-year college.

What are some alternatives to going to a four-year college?

Community college is one alternative. A trade school is another alternative. Work for a year and think about it is another alternative. Put some money in the bank. Join the military is another alternative where you earn great trade skills. We heard from an expert that there are 115,000 janitors in America with B.A.s. It's fine to be a janitor, but you didn't have to spend that kind of money to be a janitor.

Chapter 16

College Majors with the best Return on Investment

By KELSEY SHEEHY

It's no secret: College is expensive.

Nationally, student loan debt stands at $914 billion, up $10 billion from just three months prior, according to the latest quarterly report from the Federal Reserve Bank of New York.

Despite the gloom and doom over the rising cost of college, it still pays to get a degree if you do it wisely. Full-time workers with a bachelor's degree earn, on average, 84 percent more over their lifetime than those with only a high school diploma, according to a May 2011 report by the Center on Education and the Workforce at Georgetown University.

But college is an investment, and not all investments are created equal. What you study impacts the economic value your degree will hold after graduation, which is why some parents urge their students to study business instead of poetry.

In fact, 42 percent of parents say they prodded their student to pick a collegiate path based on earning potential, and 16 percent of parents say they will have their child change majors to earn more money, according to Fidelity Investments, which surveyed nearly 2,400 families for its August 2012 report.

Which majors are parents pushing their kids to pursue? Computer science, nursing, engineering, psychology, biology, and accounting, the Fidelity report states.

While engineering and computer science consistently rate among the top-paying college majors, students should also research employment demand and hot skillsets, says Andrea Porter, communications director at Georgetown's CEW.

Those skills include the ability to analyze and make sense of data, work through economic models, or understand what drives people to buy. Factoring in workforce demand, employment potential, starting salaries, and income growth can help college students ensure they get the best return on their investment.

An analytical edge

Engineering, physics, computer science, and mathematics boast strong earning potential and low unemployment rates, which can help you reap the highest return on your education investment, says Katie Bardaro, a lead economist at PayScale, an online salary database.

"Not everyone is cut out for the analytical stuff. If you are one of those people, you're lucky, because people want to hire you," Bardaro says.

With average starting salaries hovering close to $98,000 per year, a median salary of $120,000, and 95 percent of graduates employed full time, petroleum engineering majors can expect a solid return on their degree, according to PayScale salary data and a report by the CEW. The same goes for students majoring in geological engineering, a niche degree that yields high salaries and nearly 100 percent employment for majors, the CEW report says.

Engineering majors dominate most top 10 lists for degrees with a high return on investment. Here's how other engineering degrees stack up in order of median mid-career pay, according to earnings data from PayScale:

- Chemical engineering—median starting pay: $64,500; median mid-career pay: $109,000

- Electrical engineering—median starting pay: $61,300; median mid-career pay: $103,000

- Materials science and engineering—median starting pay: $60,400; median mid-career pay: $103,000

- Aerospace engineering—median starting pay: $60,700; median mid-career pay: $102,000

- Computer engineering—median starting pay: $61,800; median mid-career pay: $101,000

Long-term earning

Parents urging their students to change majors for a higher payout anticipate their child will earn more than $70,000 per year after graduation, but the average starting salary for college graduates in 2012 was less than $44,500, according to the Fidelity survey.

But students and parents should consider the lifetime earning potential of a given major when trying to determine its return on investment.

"[In] nursing, you get paid really well in the beginning, but then you just don't grow much in your career," says PayScale's Bardaro.

Graduates with degrees in physics, economics, or statistics often enter the workforce with lower initial salaries, but the potential for income growth and the flexible skillset makes these degrees solid investments, Bardaro says.

Physics lands among the top 10 majors for median pay and for growth between mid- and long-term career salaries. The same is true for economics majors, she points out.

"A lot of people talk about majoring in business ... actually, economics is even better, because you learn a lot more quantitative analysis, a lot more statistics, and things that are applicable in kind of this big data world," she says. "Similar to physics, it's really good for salary growth overall."

Here's what starting and mid-career salaries look like for these majors, according to salary data from PayScale:

- Physics—median starting pay: $49,800; median mid-career pay: $101,000

- Economics—median starting pay: $47,300; median mid-career pay: $94,700

- Statistics—median starting pay: $49,000; median mid-career pay: $93,800

Value-added skills

Majoring in a STEM subject—science, technology, engineering, and math—is not for everyone. Students working toward degrees in the humanities and social sciences can still get a strong return on their investments.

"Whether it be sociology, or political science, or anthropology ... anything that helps you understand people's behaviors and trends in behaviors, I think those would be good majors for people who aren't as analytically focused," Bardaro says.

While the salaries for these majors are lower than those for economics or engineering degrees, students can still earn strong salaries and have the versatility to work across multiple industries. Here's what starting and median salaries look like for students graduating with certain bachelor's degrees in the social sciences:

- Government—median starting pay: $41,400; median mid-career pay: $87,300

- Political science—median starting pay: $39,900; median mid-career pay: $80,100

- International relations—median starting pay: $40,500; median mid-career pay: $79,400

- Advertising—median starting pay: $37,700; median mid-career pay: $74,700

Students with the elusive combination of communications and technical skills are also in high demand, Porter, with CEW, says.

"Research what skills are most valuable in the labor market … and depending on those 'hot skills' you can also obtain a certificate that will provide you skills that will set you apart," Porter adds.

Relevant certifications, concentration areas, and minors can all add value to your degree. Choosing schools wisely can also help students get the best return on their investments, says PayScale's Bardaro.

"If you're in one of the STEM majors ... you can justify going to a more expensive school because they pay better and there's more job opportunities," she says, noting that attending a top-tier school such as Stanford University or the Massachusetts Institute of Technology can add more value to certain degrees. "If you have more interest in art or humanities ... then you should probably think about going to a cheaper school."

Chapter 17

Kick Off College Saving Before a Child is Born

By REYNA GOBEL

Brian and Elisa Keller's unborn child doesn't have a name yet – but does have a college savings account.

The Washington couple opened a GradSave account, which allows family and friends to donate money online to a college fund, because many people wanted to contribute to their child's future.

Registry services such as GradSave allow parents to transfer money accumulated on the gifting site into a 529 plan account, a tax-advantaged college investment account, of their choosing.

The Kellers aren't the only ones getting an early start. According to GradSave spokesman Eddie Pradel, it's common for parents to open GradSave accounts before a child is born in anticipation of events such as baby showers.

Gift accounts, which can be for anyone, don't require a name or social security number to open. In the account the Kellers opened, their son is "Little Man Keller," and his photo is an ultrasound image.

But 529 plans are a bit more complicated. Opening a 529 plan account requires the social security number of the beneficiary, the person entitled to use the money in the account.

Parents who want to start saving for an unborn child's college tuition typically tackle the social security number problem in one of two ways. "Some parents open a 529 plan before the baby is born in their own name and transfer the gifts there," says Pradel. "After the baby is born and they receive a social security number, they then change the beneficiary of the 529 plan to the child."

Colorado-based financial planner Mitch O'Hare started a 529 plan account for his daughter before she was born. He designated himself as both the account owner and beneficiary. Once his daughter had a social security number, he changed the beneficiary to her.

The other way parents handle the social security number problem is to leave gifts received from a baby shower or other event in a GradSave account until the baby is born, says the registry's Pradel, and open a 529 plan in the baby's name once the child has a social security number, then transfer the gifts. The Kellers have already selected the 529 plan they will open once the baby is born and has a social security number.

O'Hare encourages his clients to start saving for college before their children are born.

"Why not just start funding a 529 plan early?" he says. An earlier start means parents have more time for compound interest to accrue.

He predicts parents of children born today will need $150,000 for four years of education at a state school.

If parents are able to earn 8 percent annual interest on their investments, they could accumulate roughly $150,000 by contributing $310 per month for 18 years. If they wait 10 years to start saving for college, the monthly contribution would be have to be $1,100 to get close to that amount.

Parents saving $100 per month from the time the baby is born could save for nearly a third of their child's cost of attendance.

Would-be parents who want to get a jump on college savings should be careful, however, about starting a 529 plan if they have yet to conceive. For varying reasons, sometimes plans to have children don't work out. While the money in a 529 plan can be used for other family members such as nieces and nephews or for the parents themselves, there is a 10 percent tax penalty, plus income tax on earnings, if the money is later withdrawn for a non-educational purpose, he says.

For the Kellers, having an option to fund their child's education before birth was about continuing a family legacy.

"Both of us received savings bonds growing up from family members that paid for our education," Brian Keller says. "There's only so many things we need for our nursery. Having a baby shower registry that includes college savings feels like the right thing to do for our son."

Chapter 18

Weigh Coverdell Accounts and IRAs for College Savings Flexibility

By REYNA GOBEL

Mark Berg used to save for his child's education in a Coverdell Education Savings Account, a tax-deferred investment account for saving for both early education and college.

But the account just didn't keep up with the rising cost of college, says the Illinois-based financial planner. At the time, Coverdell accounts were limited to $500 annual contributions, totaling $9,000 in maximum contributions.

But now that the annual deposit limit for Coverdell accounts has increased to $2,000, Berg's feelings have changed. The accounts offer more flexibility in investment choices than 529 plans, another type of tax-advantaged college savings accounts.

"If you're not going to be able to contribute more than $2,000, the Coverdell makes all kinds of sense," he says.

In rare circumstances, Roth IRAs can also make sense for parents who aren't sure if their children will go to college, Berg says. Money can be withdrawn from individual retirement accounts for education tax-free, but parents can use the money for their own retirement if their child doesn't end up going to college.

While 529 plan investment choices are limited to a selection of investment choices dictated by the state, Coverdell accounts and IRAs aren't, Berg says. Account owners can choose any and as many investments as they want, from stocks to bonds and money markets.

In addition, changes in investments can be made more than once per year, which comes in handy during rises and falls in the stock market, Berg says.

For instance, when the market fell in 2008, most mutual funds containing stocks lost some cash value. In that situation, it would make sense to sell some bonds to buy stocks or stock-market based mutual funds while prices are still low.

Trying to react once a year can be like trying to buy items you saw at an after-Christmas sale in February. "They're just no longer on the shelf," he says.

A major difference between 529 plans, Coverdell Education Savings Accounts and retirement accounts are the annual contribution limits for each kind of account. The limits for 529 plans are based on the amount states deem necessary for a student's future qualified education expenses, while Coverdells are capped at $2,000 in annual contributions.

Another difference between the types of accounts is that there are income limits for tax-free contributions to Coverdell Education Savings Accounts, which don't apply to 529 plan accounts. Married couples filing joint federal taxes can't get a tax break on contributions if their combined income tops $220,000, while taxpayers with other filing statuses can't contribute tax-free if their income is above $110,000, says Ernie Almonte, a Rhode Island-based personal financial specialist and certified public accountant.

The accounts also differ in what levels of education they can be used to pay for. Coverdell accounts give parents the flexibility to pay for either primary or higher education. That makes the accounts, in conjunction with a 529 plan, useful for parents sending their children to private schools before they go to college, experts say.

Like Coverdell accounts, Roth IRA contributions are capped. Account holders less than 50 years old are currently limited to $5,500 per year, while those ages 50 and older can contribute $6,500 per year, according to the IRS.

Any IRA is technically supposed to be used as a retirement account, but there is an exception that allows account holders to withdraw money for higher education. But the money in that account has to cover retirement, too.

The federal tax rules state that withdrawals for qualified higher education expenses, such as tuition and textbooks, are not subject to the 10 percent additional tax on early withdrawals from retirement accounts. However, the money must be withdrawn for the education of immediate family members: parents or their children.

"I try to encourage clients to keep IRAs for retirement purposes," says Almonte, who used 529 plans to save for college for all five of his sons. "There are loans for college expenses but there are not many loan options for retirement."

While 529 plan rules limit families to using funds only for higher education – or else face a tax penalty – using money saved in an IRA could eat into a parent's retirement fund, so student loans are often a better solution for families.

"Parents should be careful to not overextend themselves," says student loan expert Heather Jarvis. "Federal student loans are a safe way to borrow for student expenses as long as families only borrow what they need and can afford to repay."

Chapter 19

4 Overlooked Ways to Pay for College

By KATY HOPKINS

Paying for college is rarely easy. Ideally, it's a longterm process of building and using a collection of savings, institutional aid, free money, and—if necessary—loans.

But with so many avenues for financing your education, it's often difficult to sort out what might work best for you, given your situation and time frame. Whether you'll be moving into your dorm room in two months or you're starting to save now for your toddler's college education, here are four often-overlooked considerations that may lessen your financial burden:

Exhaust your federal options: Because federal loans (Stafford and Perkins) are cheaper and have more flexible repayment options, students with financial need should always exhaust their federal options before looking to private loans, says Kevin Walker, cofounder and CEO of SimpleTuition.com. It's an often overlooked route, he adds, because some families mistakenly assume it's a complicated process for a loan they may be too well off to qualify for anyway.

"Some families might believe, 'We're upper middle class; our income is upper level so we wouldn't qualify,'" Walker notes. "Whether you're Bill Gates's kid or a child of a family with zero income, you can get a federal Stafford loan."

And, if college is around the corner and you've yet to apply for federal aid, it's also a mistake to assume you're too late, Walker notes. You can still fill out the FAFSA and work with your college's financial aid office to evaluate your payment options. Sites such as SimpleTuition, the Department of Education, and Sallie Mae offer more information on federal loans and help students navigate the private loan sector, if necessary.

Consider 529 plans: If you have some time before college, a 529 savings plan may be an attractive route for you. Named after Section 529 of the Internal Revenue Code under which it was created, a 529 plan allows users to select from a variety of funds in which to invest, including real estate and money market accounts. In 34 states and the District of Columbia, parents with a 529 plan qualify for an income tax deduction or credit on contributions.

These savings plans with tax advantages were effectively created to lessen the number of investment choices families have to make, says Mark Kantrowitz, founder of FinAid.org. But it seems the message hasn't been fully communicated; in a recent parent survey conducted by Sallie Mae, about half of all respondents who aren't using a 529 plan didn't know the option existed. That lack of information was the most commonly cited reason parents didn't use the college savings plan, according to the 2010 study, *How America Saves for College,* which surveyed 2,092 parents around the country with children under the age of 18.

"This is not rocket science," Kantrowitz says, adding that parents and students should be able to navigate the options. Ideally, a 529 savings account will be opened when a child is young, so savings can accrue over time according to an age-based investment allocation. Then, any risky investments have a decade or more to recover.

Though 529 plans—and the accompanying fees—vary by state, eligibility is not determined by residency. You can opt to enroll in Ohio's plan if you live in Virginia, for example. Consider your state's plan first, Kantrowitz recommends, then look elsewhere if its fees aren't lower than 1 percent or if it doesn't offer an attractive income tax deduction.

Regiment yourself: No matter how far away college is for you or your child, it's crucial to start adhering to a savings plan now. Though it might feel painful at first, research shows that students and parents who stow away set levels of college cash at specific intervals are more inclined to feel confident about their ability to pay for college.

"It's something called perceived self control: When people save regularly, they start to really feel that they have greater control over their lives and their future, and it leads them to build a much higher level with capability in dealing with financial matters and their financial future," says Ben Mangan, president and CEO of EARN, a financial aid nonprofit organization, which founded MyDebtStory.com.

To make the process easier, get yourself on a manageable plan, focus on the savings goal each month rather than the large end figure, and have your savings stowed away automatically, FinAid's Kantrowitz advises. "Once you get started," he says, "you become accustomed to not spending that money."

Explore last-minute options: If you are beginning college this fall, don't assume it's too late to find scholarships, SimpleTuition's Walker says. Use these next few weeks to scour the Internet, community listings, and your high school's counseling office for any last-minute sources of aid or scholarship money that went unused in the traditional school year award period. Other scholarships have deadlines throughout the calendar year. In an online scholarship search, specify what state you live in to help you find local results, Walker recommends.

Students can also use the Web to find summer contests, such as the one being held through July on Mangan's site, MyDebtStory.com. In an effort to create a community of financial aid users, the newly launched Web site is offering $5,000 to the highest user-rated video of how to pay for college. If you have other tips not listed, the site welcomes video success stories of students who have mastered the financial aid process, too.

Though these types of contests won't garner money for the majority of students who enter, the process can at least be informative—and possibly therapeutic, Mangan notes. "We've found that people sometimes feel hopeless about this," he says. "The simple act of sharing their story and knowing they're not alone gives them a sense of relief from the burden they feel in carrying the education debt."

Chapter 20

How Parents Can Stretch College Savings for Students Living at Home

By REYNA GOBEL

New York City mom Veronica Defonso carefully saved for her daughter's education, but she doesn't want to use up those funds before her child gets to graduate school. "Graduate school is absolutely necessary to get my daughter that much farther ahead," she says.

To stretch out the savings in her 529 plan, a tax-advantaged college investment account, her daughter will live at home during her first two undergraduate years. The average cost for room and board in 2012-2013 is $9,341, according to data reported by 1,063 ranked schools in an annual *U.S. News* survey. By having his or her child live at home for two years, a parent could save more than $18,000, depending on the college selected.

Parents with students choosing to live at home should follow these four tips to stretch their savings.

1. Set educational goals together to limit excess spending: While their kids are still living at home, parents should have discussions with them about their career goals and the college credits needed to achieve those goals, Arkansas 529 Plan Project Coordinator Dale Ellis says.

Saving money by living at home won't help family finances if there isn't a plan for students to graduate with degrees in a timely manner, he notes.

Map out the full plan with students' high school counselors and solidify goals via career exploration options, such as shadow days or internships, he suggests. While students might change their minds, parents should make sure current goals are based on careful research.

2. Increase investment earnings for students planning to attend grad school: The longer parents wait to tap 529 plan funds, the more time they have to grow. "If parents have limited resources and feel grad school is a definite, keep the money invested or saved while paying for [college] expenses from the parents' regular paycheck or savings account for those first two years," says Jason Washo, a certified public accountant and personal financial specialist in Arizona.

Hypothetically, this gives their 529 plans more time to grow tax free, provided funds are used for qualifying educational expenses. However, this only works if the students eventually attend graduate school, he notes. Otherwise, there may be tax penalties for withdrawing excess funds if the money isn't transferred to an eligible beneficiary.

3. Use matching grant funds wisely: To avoid losing benefits, parents in states that offer 529 plan matching grants shouldn't wait to use those funds unless it's definite that their child will go to graduate school, Ellis says.

For instance, an Arkansas couple may have earned up to $2,500 in matching contributions for their child, but saved those funds for graduate school. Instead, the couple spent their own funds or borrowed money to pay for college. After earning an undergraduate degree, the child decided not to continue schooling. Since matching grants are only payable to a university, the matching grants expired unused.

4. Watch kids' student loan borrowing habits: "Often, students living at home borrow more in student loans than needed to pay for educational expenses," Ellis says. Therefore, it's important for parents to help their kids budget for college expenses.

For example, a student gets a $2,000 student loan refund check after tuition and fees are deducted. Textbooks cost $400; with $1,600 left, the student then buys music downloads and extra clothing, and goes out with friends. After four semesters, the student owes $6,400 that he or she didn't need to borrow. Interest may also accrue.

Parents should talk to their kids about taking out fewer student loans, Ellis says. If students are swallowed by debt when they graduate, this ultimately defeats the purpose of parents saving for college.

Chapter 21

8 Ways to Save Money on College Textbooks

By Robert Berger

College students spend an average of $655 per year on textbooks, according to the National Association of College Stores. Even though this figure is down from two and four years ago – from $667 and $702, respectively – it's still a lot of money, especially for broke college students.

Depending on your major, your average book expense may be much more or much less than $655. Hefty textbooks used in math and science classes, for instance, tend to be more expensive than novels needed for literature classes. Still, no matter your course of study, you can apply some of these basic tips to save on college textbooks.

1. Steer clear of the bookstore. This is the No. 1 one way to spend less money on textbooks. Shopping at the college bookstore for textbooks is akin to picking up all your groceries at the corner gas station. Convenience, in both cases, means higher prices. You may need to pick up some specialized materials in your bookstore, like packets printed out by a professor for a

specific class, but most of the time you can – and should – shop elsewhere for your books.

2. Buy used. College students have been buying used textbooks for years, and they shouldn't stop now. Buying used books can save you a fortune, and often, the books are in good condition. You may be tempted to just pick up used books from your bookstore, but you can often find better prices online.

The easiest way to shop for used books online is to use ISBN numbers. These numbers are specific, so you'll get the exact book and edition your class is using. Websites such as Amazon, eBay and book.ly are great places to shop around. MyNextCollege.com also offers a free search tool that compares prices from dozens of online stores.

3. Share. One option that works for some courses is simply to share. Split the cost with a roommate or close friend taking the same class, and share the book. As long as you can arrange study schedules so that you both get the book as often as you need it, this can work out well. Some professors are adamant that students have their books available during class, while others use the texts as supplemental reading and focus class time on lectures. Figuring out a professor's style before you decide to share textbooks may be a good idea.

4. Check the library. While your school library may not have a copy of every single textbook, it's likely to have copies of some

of them – especially fiction and non-fiction books for liberal arts classes. The key to using the library is to ensure you can get the books when you need them. Ordering books ahead of time or using the interlibrary loan system can help. But you might want to keep some backup cash in case you can't get the book at the library and need to buy a copy.

5. Rent books. Renting books is becoming a more popular option and can be a good way to save. Rentals are especially popular for the most expensive books, like math and science texts. If you want to rent books, you will likely have to deal with your campus bookstore, but this is one case that makes sense to do so.

First, you need to make sure you understand the terms of the rental. You may need to take extra care of rental books so you don't lose money when you return them. And take time to see how much a used version of the book would sell for, as it might make more sense financially to buy the book and then resell it later. Finally, be aware that renting is not always the cheapest option, particularly when you factor in the resale value of a textbook you buy.

6. Opt for ebooks. Many textbooks are now available in ebook format, and you can buy or rent them in this cheaper format as long as you have an e-reader. If you're taking classes that require historical texts, fiction, biographies, poetry and essays, you'll likely find those texts in ebook format. One key to

success with ebooks is to make sure you can easily navigate the book. Sometimes it's more difficult to find a particular page using an ebook, which can be frustrating when participating in a seminar that involves jumping around by page number.

7. Consider buying the older edition. The California Student Public Interest Research Group published a study in 2004 that found new editions cost 58 percent more than older editions. Newer editions are often not that different from previous editions – they just sometimes look nicer and have different page numbers. You will want to compare old and new editions to ensure there aren't any major differences between them, and you'll be prepared to hunt down information during lectures, since your page numbers will probably be different.

8. Decide which you'll use long-term. Once in a blue moon, it's a good idea to buy a brand new textbook, even if you have to pay full price. This isn't normally the case for introductory classes, as you'll likely never use those books again. But once you get into the upper-level courses for your major, those textbooks could come in handy during your future career. Think carefully about which books you might use over the long term, and consider purchasing just those books new. That way, you'll get a book without several students' worth of wear and tear.

Chapter 22

5 Big Financial Aid Lies

By KIM CLARK

One of the reasons students and parents are so frustrated by their attempts to figure out how to pay for college is that many of the terms that government officials and college administrators use can be misleading.

In eight years of researching and writing about financial aid, I have met and interviewed hundreds, if not thousands, of the college and government officials who create and enforce financial aid rules. And the vast majority of them have seemed to me to be honorable, idealistic people. But too often they end up misleading students or parents because many of the financial aid terms they have to use turn out to have technical or legal definitions that run directly counter to commonly understood meanings. And in some cases, I believe, politicians or college officials have purposely crafted terms that give students more hope for aid than is realistic. I realize that calling something a "lie" is inflammatory. Before you post any blistering comments, consider these financial aid terms and draw your own conclusions:

1. "Expected Family Contribution": The federal government calculates what it calls an "Expected Family Contribution" for students who complete a Free Application for Federal Student Aid. Anyone with access to a dictionary would conclude that means the government has figured out how much the student's family should be "expected" to "contribute" to the student's college expenses.

Many students and parents get unpleasant surprises when the government sends them their EFC because the government's formula for figuring out what families should be able to afford is unrealistic. The federal government expects parents to contribute at least 22 (and, for wealthier families, as much as 47) cents of every dollar above an arbitrarily low family budget. For example, a single working mother would be expected to start contributing for every dollar she earns above about $30,000 a year. That means a mom who makes about $50,000 a year could be expected to "contribute" more than $3,000 a year to her student's college expenses. But if that mother happens to live in an expensive city such as New York, Boston or San Francisco, she's probably spending half her take-home pay on rent alone. Add in necessities such as transportation, health insurance, and food and the Economic Policy Institute's "Basic Family Budget

Calculator," shows that there often isn't $300 left at the end of the year, let alone $3,000.

The EFC is further undermined when students go to college. More than 97 percent of colleges don't have enough financial aid money to guarantee that every student will only have to pay their EFC. The average public four-year college tells families earning about $56,000 a year that they have to kick in about $2,000 more than the federal government's "Expected Family Contribution." [See the list of colleges that claim they provide enough aid to meet a family's need.] Many colleges award big scholarships to the students they are trying to lure because of athletic skills or top grades. So yes, the government does calculate a contribution that it thinks families should contribute to college costs. But that expectation is often painfully unrealistic. And the percentage of students whose college bills actually match their EFC is surprisingly small. Many talented students end up paying less than their EFC. And millions of less fortunate students are, unhappily, expected to contribute much more than their often unaffordable EFC. Justin Draeger, the National Association of Student Financial Aid Administrators' vice president for public policy, confirms: "the EFC that tells you nothing. It doesn't tell you how much you're going to have to pay...The whole thing is broken." Of course, the best fix would be to provide enough aid so that students could actually afford college. But in these cash-strapped times, a no-cost improvement would be to call that number something like "Family Financial Strength Indicator," and thus stop giving students the false impression that the EFC is what they will be expected to pay.

2. "Guaranteed" or "conservative" college savings plans: Some state college savings plans have been giving parents too rosy a view of their chances of saving enough for college. OppenheimerFunds, for example, has agreed to pay out millions of dollars to settle charges that it marketed as "conservative," some 529 savings plans that plunged in value because they were actually packed with leveraged toxic securities. And some states marketing college savings plans "guaranteed" to keep up with inflation, are backpedaling on those promises. Texas's now-closed Guaranteed Tuition Plan, for example, last year stopped paying investors who wanted refunds the originally promised value of all the investors' contributions plus all investment gains. Now, those who want a refund get only their actual investments minus administrative fees. Several other state "guaranteed" savings plans are backed by surprisingly flimsy "guarantees." Pennsylvania's legislature created a "Guaranteed" savings plan that is "guaranteed" by nothing more than the fund itself, for example In several other states, the "guarantee" turns out to be nothing more than the promise that if the savings plan gets into financial trouble, the executives are "guaranteed" to ask the state legislature for a bailout. The legislature, of course, is free to say no. Increasingly, college savings plans are trying to alert

investors to their risks and unique definitions. Pennsylvania's website, for example, makes clear that there is no real backup to the guarantee. But wouldn't it be simpler and more accurate to give the funds names that don't have to be explained with lots of footnotes and disclaimers?

3. "Teach Grant": This federal financial aid program for aspiring teachers offers forgivable loans, not outright grants. The recipients who fail to jump through lots of hoops, including spending several years teaching specified subjects at schools certain schools , end up getting bills for their "Teach Grants" plus interest. Some college financial aid officials feel the program is so misleading that they refuse to process students' applications. "The name is the problem," says Ted Malone, who heads the financial aid office at the University of Alaska, and who refuses to process TEACH Grant applications for freshmen and sophomores. "I really do think that if they just called it what it really is—a forgivable loan—more people might be interested, and people would be going in with their eyes wide open."

4. "7.9% federal PLUS loans": When advertising loans, lenders such as credit card companies and used car dealers must give consumers plenty of warning about the true annual percentage rate (APR). That means that the lender must add all the extra fees to the annual interest rate. The federal government doesn't use APRs in its general information about its graduate or parent PLUS loans, however. The government does make clear

that it typically charges a 4 percent upfront fee for PLUS loans. But it doesn't give borrowers much heads up that those fees mean the true APR on a 10-year, $10,000 PLUS loan turns out to be 8.8 percent.

5. "Renewable" merit scholarships: Most schools and organizations tell scholarship winners the rules they'll need to follow and grades they'll need to achieve to renew their scholarships in future years. But only a few organizations give prospective, and, all too often, overconfident, students any statistics or warning of the odds of their receiving merit scholarships for all four years. Some officials in states such as Georgia and Tennessee warn high-schoolers that as many as half of the B students who earn Hope Scholarships drop below a B average in their freshman year, and thus lose their merit scholarships for sophomore year. But some schools have set much higher and tougher hurdles—GPAs of 3.5, or even 3.8—for other merit scholarships, and don't always warn the winners about previous recipients' records of achieving those kinds of grades over four years.

Chapter 23

4 Steps to Financially Prepare Your Student for College

By KATY HOPKINS

Heading off to freshman year of college is a gateway to new experiences—a time to explore academic interests, meet new people, and, for some students, embrace newfound financial independence.

"Sometimes, this is the first time that they're actually starting to manage money on their own, without their parents being right there with them to help them along the way," says Doug Schantz, director of the Office of Student Accounts at Ohio's Wittenberg University and founder of CheapScholar.org. "For those of us who have been managing our finances, you assume that this is basic financial information—but the fact of the matter is, it really isn't."

For parents, preparing your student to be financially successful in college is a delicate balance between supplying enough funds and know-how for your child to get by and becoming so overly involved that he or she can't fully flourish, both personally and financially. Here's what to brief your students on before they head off to school—and what you should let your children learn on their own:

1. Don't deposit and dash: For parents who plan to supply their student with extra spending money, realize that your offer is both incredibly generous and potentially hazardous, if you're doling out a semester or year's worth of cash without a loose framework of how that money should be divided, notes Houston Dougharty, vice president of student affairs at Grinnell College in Iowa. "Too often, I have worked with [parents] who, upon dropping off their student, say, 'I've put $2,000 in your checking account for the year,'—and then that student is the most generous pizza buyer for the first month of college," Dougharty says. "[By] October, they don't have money to do laundry."

Instead, talk to your students about the importance of intentional, incremental budgeting. Help them set up a month-to-month plan that allows for unexpected expenses, such as an off-campus dinner with hall mates or a few extra loads of wash. That conversation is also a great opportunity to be honest about what they can assume from you; if you expect your student to save money to cover the last two years of tuition, for example, or if he or she will be paying for textbooks out of pocket, mention that now, experts recommend.

2. Embrace—and limit—financial slip-ups: After helping with a budget framework, step out of the process and leave it to your son or daughter to make it work, recommends Jerry Weichman, a clinical psychologist in Newport Beach, Calif. "If your kid runs out of money [one] month, they're not going to starve—they can buy some Ramen," Weichman says. "One of the best things parents can do is to allow your kids to struggle financially for a little bit if they mismanage their money, because the consequences are so much easier for them now versus what that would equate to when they're adults. You learn so much more from your mistakes than your successes."

Still, parents who remove themselves don't have to leave their students completely helpless. "You can put limits on how dangerous financial experiences can be," notes June Walbert, financial planner at USAA Financial Planning Services. Encourage your student to get a debit card or a credit card with a low spending limit, she recommends, and recap his or her financial experience together at the end of each semester or school year. "Much of the learning during college happens outside the confines of the classroom, especially on the personal finance front," Walbert says. "We want students to be free to make financial decisions, but within boundaries."

3. Encourage financial freedom: Often, a part-time job—usually for about 10 hours a week—can help increase a student's productivity, organization, and time management skills, claims

Grinnell College's Dougharty, in addition to providing a little financial leeway. If your student works, suggest the earnings be used as spending money—whether he or she chooses to put it toward laundry, occasional meals off campus, or extracurricular activities—rather than set costs such as tuition or room and board, Dougharty recommends. By choosing where to allocate earnings, students actively make a connection between money earned and money spent, and will likely be more effective at budgeting after college since, Dougharty says, "That's what real life is like."

4. Utilize web resources: Though releasing the tether from your soon-to-be college student may still be a terrifying thought, rest assured that neither you nor your student needs to tackle the upcoming challenges alone. With the help of the Internet, students have financial management resources at their fingertips. Check out Mint.com for help with your budget, recommends Katherine Cohen, founder of Ivywise.com; explore the government-run MyMoney.gov for advice on making informed financial decisions; or see if your school has a virtual financial literacy program that makes money issues fun and understandable, such as the program Schantz is currently implementing at Wittenberg University.

And if it gets tough making the shift from "daily parent to occasional coach," as Grinnell's Dougharty puts it, keep in mind that, after years of personal training within your family unit, allowing your student some leeway is a healthy route to tackling problems in school and beyond.

"Money management, conserving, saving for what you need, and tracking your expenses are parts of what any adult needs to be successful, let alone a college student," counselor Weichman says. "Parents are teaching their kids not just how to deal with college, but how to deal with life."

Chapter 24

4 Questions to Ask During Student Loan Counseling

By KELSEY SHEEHY

College student loan counseling leaves a lot to be desired, according to students and experts.

"It simply involved checking off boxes saying that I agree to certain terms," Simon Tam, an MBA student at Marylhurst University in Oregon, said via email. "There is no opportunity to interact at all."

Counseling for federal student loans, such as Stafford and PLUS loans, typically takes place online. The format requires students to scroll through a Web page that lays out how their loans are disbursed, how interest accrues and when repayment begins, among other things.

Borrowers then have to answer questions such as "What is the interest rate on a subsidized Stafford loan?" or "Are student loans dischargeable in bankruptcy?" says KC Deane, a research associate at the American Enterprise Institute's Center on Higher Education Reform.

"These very basic questions that students should know," says Deane. "The problem is that because it is this bizarre process of taking an online quiz that you don't have to study for, because the answers are right there, it just doesn't stick."

While students may be tempted to blow through their automated loan counseling, finding answers to key questions throughout the process can save them major headaches down the road, experts say.

Below are four questions students should have answers to before signing off on their student loan entrance counseling, even if it means they have to talk to a real person.

1. How much am I borrowing? This may seem like an obvious question, but few student borrowers truly grasp the amount they are taking out.

"It's treated too much like free money," Deane says.

Students should ensure they have a clear understanding not only of how much they borrow that first year, but how much they can expect to borrow over the course of their degree, Jim Anderson, director of financial aid at Montclair State University, said via email.

As a rule of thumb, students should cap their debt based on future earnings, says Mitchell Weiss, an adjunct professor of finance at the University of Hartford.

"You don't want to borrow more than what you can reasonably expect to earn," says Weiss, who is also cofounder of the university's Center for Personal Financial Responsibility.

Students can ensure their monthly loan payments don't exceed 10 percent of their income by keeping the total amount borrowed at or below the average first-year earnings for their degree field, he advises.

"That is really important because that will let you not live in your parents' basement," Weiss says.

2. What about interest and fees? Interest rates vary from student loan to student loan. When that interest will start accruing is also dependent on the type of loan.

Federal Perkins loans charge no interest while a student is in school, but they begin accumulating interest nine months after a student leaves school at a rate of 5 percent annually. Stafford loans come with an upfront fee of 0.5 percent and interest rates of 6.8 percent a year. Unsubsidized Stafford loans start compiling interest right away, but the subsidized version does not start tacking on the extra percentage until after a student leaves school.

"The subsidized, unsubsidized difference is a huge deal," says Deane, who points out the first student loan bill can be a shock for students."With service fees and interest having accrued over the last however many years, they now owe a lot more than they thought at the front end."

3. Who is my lender? Student loans come in many forms and from several lenders. Where the money is coming from – the state, university, federal government or private lender – will determine important details such as interest rates, grace periods and repayment options, Deane, says.

It will also dictate who is sending you the bill.

Federal loans such as the Stafford and Parent PLUS loans are serviced by the Department of Education's Direct loan program. But Perkins loans, though technically federal loans, are often serviced by the university. Some states run lending programs, as well.

So without even taking out private loans, students could be tasked with keeping tabs on three separate loan statements and payment due dates, all housed on different websites. That means updating your address, signing up for electronic billing and negotiating repayment options three different times, Deane points out.

4. Where can I go to find this information when I need it? The timing of student loan counseling isn't ideal, Allesandra

Lanza with American Student Assistance, a nonprofit focused on student debt, said via email.

"Counseling four years or more before repayment starts doesn't work," Lanza wrote. "Even exit counseling is six months before repayment starts – a lifetime for a recent college grad."

Even if students read through all of their loan documents, it's unlikely they will retain everything years down the road.

To ensure they have access to vital information – interest rates, repayment plans and consolidation and forgiveness options – borrowers should ask their financial aid adviser where they can easily access all of those details throughout the life of their student loans.

Chapter 25

Parent Plus Loans: Frequently Asked Questions

By U.S. News Staff

What is a parent PLUS loan?

A federally guaranteed parent loan that can be used to cover your child's higher education costs.

How much can I borrow from the PLUS program?

Each year, parents can borrow the full out-of-pocket cost of each child's annual college education. To calculate the maximum PLUS eligibility, take the college's annual cost of attendance and subtract any other financial aid, such as grants, scholarships and other federal student loans.

How much do PLUS loans cost?

Interest rates on parent PLUS loans are now market-based, so they will fluctuate from year to year. Once the loan is issued, however, the rate is locked in. The interest rate on PLUS loans is determined using the interest rate of the 10-year Treasury note on June 1, plus 4.6 percent. Rates for PLUS loans are capped at 10.5 percent. Taxpayers with low and middle incomes can deduct their education loan interest payments, further reducing the cost of the loan.

Who makes PLUS loans?

As of July 1, 2010, only the federal government makes PLUS loans. But applications are usually processed through your child's college.

How do I get a PLUS loan?

The first step is to call the financial aid office at your student's college. It is not technically necessary for the parent to fill out a FAFSA, though many schools urge doing so to determine if students qualify for other aid, such as grants, scholarships or Stafford loans.

Does everyone get approved for a PLUS?

No. The government rejects parents who've had significant financial trouble – known as adverse credit –such as a recent bankruptcy or bills more than 90 days overdue. Parents can reapply if they can find a cosigner with good credit.

What happens if I get rejected for a PLUS?

Children of parents who have been rejected for a PLUS loan are allowed to borrow more from the Stafford program.

Are PLUS loan payments tax deductible?

It depends on your income. Generally not for two-parent families with incomes above $155,000.

When do I have to start repaying my PLUS loan?

For all PLUS loans made after July 1, 2008, borrowers can defer payments until after the student has left college. But beware, the interest is quietly building up during that time.

What happens if I lose my job or get into other financial trouble?

You can call the Department of Education and ask to apply for forbearance, which allows you to skip some payments. Interest continues to accrue during forbearance, so you'll owe a lot more when you start repaying again.

What are the advantages of a PLUS loan?

While interest rates on new PLUS loans can vary annually, once the loan is issued the rate is dixed for the duration, so your payments won't rise if interest rates rise. They also offer free insurance, so the debt will be canceled if the parent or the student dies or becomes disabled. PLUS borrowers can also get their payments deferred if they get into financial trouble.

What are the downsides of PLUS loans?

Unlike credit card debt and mortgages, which can be canceled if you file for bankruptcy, education loans of all types must be paid. Most bankruptcy courts will not cancel them unless your situation is extremely dire.

Chapter 26

6 Steps to Reducing Your Student Loan Costs

By KIM CLARK

If you can't get enough grants or scholarships, and have done all you can to reduce your costs, it may be a wise move to borrow—in moderation and carefully—for your graduate education. Studies show that graduate degrees often help boost career and earnings options. Still, because the economy is unpredictable, it's prudent to try to limit your debt. Here are some tips to reduce your graduate school debts.

1. Borrow as little as possible. Keep living expenses as low as possible and try not to borrow to fund them. Remember the old saying: If you live like a lawyer when you're a law student, you'll have to live like a law student when you're a lawyer.

2. Check out your future salary, and the earnings records of the graduates of your school, to see how much you can reasonably afford to put toward debt payments when you finish school. Use a loan repayment calculator to estimate how much that means you can afford to borrow now. If there's a good chance your payments will leave you with

very little to live on, or put your debt to income ratio out of whack, rethink your plans by looking for less expensive schools or better financial aid.

3. Look for loans with the lowest interest rates and fees available. Check with your school or charities to see if you qualify for a loan charging no interest at all.

4. Fill out the Free Application for Federal Student Aid to qualify for low-cost federal student loans. Do this before charging tuition on your credit card or signing up for a private loan.

5. Investigate the growing number of loan repayment or forgiveness programs offered by selected graduate schools, employers and professional organizations. While Loan Repayment Assistance Programs, or LRAPs, are fairly common for lawyers doing public service work, there are a growing number for medical professionals, policy grad students, and even M.B.A.'s.

6. Consolidate your federal student loans with the federal government after leaving grad school and apply for Income-Based Repayment. This new program allows debtors to cap monthly payments below 15 percent of their income. Debtors who work in public service and make 120 on-time payments can discharge their remaining debts for free. Those who keep making payments for 25 years can have their remaining debts forgiven no matter what their jobs.

Chapter 27

Consider When to Use Private Student Loans

By KATY HOPKINS

There are a few often-cited steps to take when it comes to borrowing for college. First, maximize all other sources you have to pay for college, including grants and scholarships, before even thinking about student loans, which will ultimately cost you more than the dollar amount you borrow.

Next, take as much as you can through federal loan programs, the most common lending vehicle used by students. Federal student loans include the Stafford, which comes with a low, fixed interest rate of 3.4 percent for undergraduates. To determine your eligibility for federal student loans, fill out the FAFSA and keep an eye out for loan awards in your financial aid packages.

But what happens if you still don't have enough money to pay for college? Take a step back to re-evaluate whether your college and major are the right choices for you—academically and financially. If so, consider your remaining options: the federal Parent PLUS loan and loans from private lenders.

"That is, I think, where this comparison is really key," says PK Parek, vice president of Discover Student Loans. "Both the PLUS loan and private loan can cover up to 100 percent of that gap in cost."

For eligible parents who are willing to take on debt for their student's education, Parent PLUS loans carry a fixed 7.9 percent interest rate and have a 4 percent origination fee. But the PLUS loans require a greater buy-in on the part of a student's parents, notes Joe Wilson, wealth management adviser at financial firm TIAA-CREF.

"One of the major differences is the fact that a private student loan is taken out by the student, and the obligation to repay is the student's first, versus that PLUS loan, where, essentially, the parent is on the hook first," Wilson says. "Even if the student agrees to repay, especially if they renege on that agreement, the parent is still on the hook."

Conversely, students can get private loans on their own— though often only with a credit-worthy cosigner—and the loans may come with lower rates and fees. Options offered through Discover, for instance, come with fixed rates between 6.79 and 9.99 (depending on borrower and cosigner credit history) and have a 0 percent origination fee, Parek notes.

"Some lenders are really trying to point out in the current interest rate environment that, in many cases, private loans are actually cheaper," says Patrick Kandianis, cofounder of Simple Tuition, a company that helps borrowers evaluate their private student loan options, in addition to other services. "You're starting to hear more about the differences or the benefits of private borrowing in terms of the cost structure versus some of the federal options."

Though more private lenders have begun to offer fixed rate loan options, the majority of private loans available still have variable rates, which may look attractive but can be risky. Posted private loan interest rates could be as low as the 3.2 percent offered through CitiBank, for example, but not every borrower will qualify for a rate that low. Plus, since it's variable, there is no guarantee that your interest rate won't spike before you've finished paying off your debt—ultimately costing you more.

And private loans with either fixed or variable rates have riskier repayment structures than federal loan programs. No student loan can be discharged in bankruptcy, but federal loan borrowers may be eligible for flexible repayment plans, such as Income-Based Repayment, which calibrates monthly charges to eligible borrowers' salaries, and Public Service Loan Forgiveness, which cancels any remaining debt for borrowers who have worked in the public sector for 10 years. Private loan borrowers, in comparison, do not automatically have the same protections or opportunities to cancel their debt.

Still, some safeguards have been put in place for private student loan borrowers, and the Consumer Financial Protection Bureau has made recommendations for future student loan policy changes. Now, for instance, colleges have to certify that a student is borrowing a manageable amount of debt, even among loans from private lenders. "There's been a lot of work to try to make sure that people aren't just crazy borrowing," Kandianis notes.

Borrowers are ultimately in charge of the amount of debt they take on. Research into starting salaries and employers hiring grads from your school can help you project the likelihood of what you'll be able to pay, whether you're borrowing through a federal program or a private lender. A manageable student loan repayment will be about 10 percent of your monthly take-home pay after graduation, many experts recommend.

For any type of student loan, tell yourself this, Kandianis recommends: "I'm borrowing a whole bunch of money, and the only way I'm going to repay it is if I get out and get a good job ... Am I financing a throw-away or something sturdy that's going to be around for awhile?"

Chapter 28

Consider These Options to Cut College Costs

By JUSTIN SNIDER

Brandon Hong had to figure out how to finance his education.

Interested in a military career, the San Jose, Calif., native applied for a Reserve Officers Training Corps (ROTC) scholarship from the federal government. Not only did he receive it, but the college he chose to attend—Boston University—gave him additional aid, covering virtually all of his costs. Hong majored in aerospace engineering and graduated in May 2011. He has been commissioned as a second lieutenant in the U.S. Air Force.

"ROTC is kind of like a full-time job on top of classes," Hong says. "But you learn how to manage your time." And it definitely helped that BU is "really, really supportive of the program," he adds.

Hong considered other colleges with ROTC programs—including the University of California—San Diego and George Washington University in Washington, D.C.—but their financial aid packages weren't as generous. Attending the U.S. Air Force

Academy in Colorado Springs, Colo., was another option Hong weighed, but the application process seemed burdensome, and he wanted a more typical college experience.

Hong could spend a decade or more fulfilling his commitment to the Air Force, but he is quick to see the upsides. He avoided taking out any loans at a time when the average student with loans graduates with an average of about $27,000 in debt, and he avoided job-hunting in a sluggish economy.

For most students, going to college remains an expensive proposition. The College Board reports that in 2011-2012, after adjusting for inflation, tuition and fees at public four-year universities were 3.68 times what they were in 1981-1982, while at private four-year colleges the figure was 2.81. Though financial aid can dramatically reduce the debt load, students who make smart decisions when choosing a school can reduce their costs—and not just by enrolling in ROTC.

Some other ideas:

Go to community college, then transfer: One alternative for high school grads is to attend a local community college for a year or two before transferring to a four-year institution. In California, it costs about $1,100 a year for full-time tuition at a community college versus about $12,190 within the University of California system; students can also save on room and board by living at home.

Starting out at a community college offers other advantages when the time comes to apply to a four-year school. For instance, roughly two thirds of transfer students accepted by Amherst College in Massachusetts come from community colleges. At the University of Virginia in Charlottesville, the figure is more than 40 percent.

The University of Massachusetts—Lowell helps transfer students finish their bachelor's degrees by providing up to four semesters of free tuition for those who earn associate degrees (with at least a 3.0 GPA) at one of the state's 15 community colleges. Other state university systems across the country are offering similar opportunities.

Go to an in-state school: Historically, a student who chose to go to a public university in another state has had to pay considerably higher tuition than in-staters. At the University of Michigan—Ann Arbor, for instance, in-state tuition and fees for full-time freshmen will be $12,994 in 2012-2013, compared to $39,122 for out-of-state students. At the University of North Carolina—Chapel Hill, the difference in tuition and fees is similarly large: $7,690 for residents versus $28,442 for nonresidents.

States are able to justify such discrepancies because their tax dollars are the main source of support for public universities, and policymakers feel they should be using that money to subsidize the education of students whose families are paying those taxes.

In addition, out-of-state students are less likely to stay beyond graduation and contribute to the local economy.

In recent years, some regions have adapted and expanded the in-state model. For example, in the Midwest, states have forged reciprocal agreements to give out-of-state students a break on tuition at participating institutions, from community colleges to research universities offering doctoral degrees.

The Midwest Student Exchange Program allows residents of nine states—Illinois, Indiana, Kansas, Michigan, Minnesota, Missouri, Nebraska, North Dakota, and Wisconsin—to study at participating public institutions in other member states for no more than 150 percent of the cost of in-state tuition. Some private schools are also among the program's 150-plus institutions, giving students a 10 percent discount on tuition.

Get your degree early: The most surefire way to save money is to finish college ahead of schedule. A handful of schools offer formal three-year bachelor's degrees, while many more grant credit for high scores on Advanced Placement and International Baccalaureate exams. Bates College in Lewiston, Maine, has offered a three-year bachelor's since 1965. Though only a few students choose this route each year, it remains an appealing option for some highly motivated and focused undergrads.

The AP and IB programs are widely recognized for providing a challenging pre-college experience, and high scores on their exams can also enable students to earn valuable college credits. All eight Ivy League universities permit students to apply for and receive "advanced standing," which allows them to graduate a semester or year early.

Students at Harvard University who have earned a 5—the highest possible score—on at least four yearlong AP courses can petition for advanced standing. Harvard students can also graduate ahead of schedule if they have earned the maximum score on three or more higher-level IB exams, or they can stick around to earn a master's degree in certain fields during their fourth year on campus.

Some of the more selective institutions outside the Ivy League, however, don't offer any credit for top scores on AP or IB exams, even though they like to see these courses on applicants' transcripts. Williams College in Massachusetts, for instance, permits students with superior scores to place out of certain introductory-level courses, but they still must complete eight semesters of full-time study just like any other student.

Start in high school: "Dual enrollment" is another, if lesser known, way to save money on college. The basic idea is for high school students to take college-level courses that can count first toward their diploma and, later, toward their college degree. Often, through agreements with local institutions, these courses are taught on high school campuses by high school teachers. The material, however, is meant to be on par with what's taught at college.

Portland State University in Oregon has been offering dual-credit classes to high school students for more than 35 years. About 1,000 students from 16 high schools in the Portland metropolitan area participate annually, according to program director Sally Hudson. Students pay about a third of the standard tuition rate—in 2012-2013, it will be $226 for a four-credit class, discounted from $734—but study the same materials and meet the same standards as other PSU students.

All seven institutions in the Oregon University System, as well as all of the state's public community colleges, guarantee credit for dual-enrollment classes. Because it can be difficult to determine the rigor of dual-enrollment classes, some colleges—especially smaller and private institutions—give no credit for them. One way to avoid this disappointment is to look into different colleges' policies on these programs and ensure that the classes are regionally or nationally accredited.

Chapter 29

What Does Net Price Mean?

By KATY HOPKINS

By a federal mandate, every college and university now has an online net price calculator, which you can use to estimate how much you will need to pay for college. But for the tools to be useful to parents and students, it's crucial to be aware of what is actually being calculated.

Net price, for the purposes of these calculators, is the total cost of one year of a college education for a first-time, full-time undergraduate, minus any grant aid you might receive. The new calculators estimate what need-based aid your family may be eligible for, sometimes requiring information from documents including income and tax statements, and then deduct that estimate of aid from the total cost for a full-time, first year student in a recent year. (The federal calculator template, arguably the most basic, requires some less specific information, including your parents' salary ranges, rather than precise dollar sums.)

The hope, then, is that students and parents may realize that a college with a high sticker price might be more affordable than it seems. Still, it's important to know that the estimate given by one school's calculator may be vastly different than the calculation of another, in part because of potentially different inputs.

While many schools are only deducting estimated federal need-based aid from their net price calculation totals, others may account for deductions including merit awards, scholarships, state aid, and "self-help aid," which can include potential loans and work-study programs. Calculators that give families a breakdown of what went into the estimates may be easier to understand, but that's not necessitated by the federal mandate.

It's also very important to keep in mind that your net price calculation, no matter the inputs, is only an estimate of what you'll pay if you enroll at the school. The calculators use aid data that already exists, rather than projections, so your estimate won't accurately correlate to what you might pay years in the future.

Even if you'll be starting school in the next calendar year, your actual cost may be thousands of dollars different than the calculator's estimate, as Mark Kantrowitz, founder of FinAid.org, has noted. If college is still several years away, your actual costs will likely be even more different than your calculation now, as tuition and fees rise each year at most colleges.

Even when you understand the complications and limitations of using the tools, you'll need to find a school's net price calculator before you can use it. *U.S. News* has located more than 250 net price calculators at top colleges; if you're interested in others, try checking the colleges' financial aid pages or doing site searches on school pages.

As you search, be aware that some schools are using different naming conventions for their net price calculators. Juniata College, for example, markets its net price calculator as a "Personal Cost Estimator;" on Bowling Green State University's site, the tool is called a "Student Financial Aid Estimator."

"We've seen things like 'college cost estimator,' 'financial aid estimator,' 'financial cost estimator,'" says Diane Cheng, a research associate at the nonprofit Institute for College Access and Success. "One of the things we're advising students is: keep your eyes open for those keywords as well, and not just 'net price calculator.'"

No matter the template or naming convention of the calculator you're using, make sure to read the disclaimer, and remember that these are estimates, not total sums or guarantees of either admission or financial aid.

Chapter 30

Why Prospective College Students Should Be Using Net Price Calculators

By KATY HOPKINS

While the average published tuition prices at colleges and universities have increased since the 2007-2008 school year, the average student has not shouldered the brunt of the rising costs, a new study has found.

The average in-state student at a four year public college is paying about $440 more in today's dollars for tuition and fees in the 2012-2013 school year than students did in 2007-2008, according to estimates in the College Board's "Trends in College Pricing 2012" study, released yesterday. And for students at private colleges, which tend to be more expensive, the average net price for tuition and fees decreased by $490 in inflation-adjusted dollars.

Grant aid from the federal government, state governments, and institutions themselves, in addition to education tax benefits, helped to absorb some of the tuition increases, according to the report's calculations and estimates.

Though average published in-state tuition jumped from $6,810 in 2007-2008 to $8,660 this year at four year publics, aid such as Pell grants and tax benefits helped to keep the increase in average net price for tuition and fees relatively small when comparing the two time periods. (The study notes, however, that federal aid was "unusually large" from 2008-2009 to 2010-2011, and that net tuition price has increased annually since.)

At private schools, published tuition rose from an average of $25,760 to $29,060 over the five years but was accompanied by more institutional aid—demonstrating that sticker prices don't always tell the full story to prospective students and their parents.

"Although it is generally the published prices that make headlines, it is the net prices paid by individual students that matter most for college access and affordability," write study authors Jennifer Ma and Sandy Baum.

As the report notes, not every student will be charged the average net price for tuition. According to the College Board, about one third of students pay a school's published tuition price in full. Prospective college students and their parents can estimate their own cost of college by using net price calculators—tools which, by federal mandate, every college is required to post online.

"It's important that families look at what's been happening to average net prices; but they also, for those close to college age, should look at specific institutions and apply their own financial situation to see what their expected net price will be," College Board author Ma recommends.

The calculators require time, knowledge of family finances, and, often, some paperwork as families work to ballpark total costs. While the College Board statistics cited above focus solely on net tuition and fees, college net price calculators take into account the total cost of college for one year, including room, board, and other expenses, when creating individual estimates.

Net price calculators aren't always easy to find. In a random sample of 50 colleges, about 25 percent of schools did not include a way to access the calculator on their financial aid websites, according to "Adding It All Up 2012: Are College Net Price Calculators Easy to Find, Use, and Compare?," a report from The Institute for College Access and Success (TICAS).

"Net price calculators are one of several new tools that can help bring more transparency to the process of deciding where to apply and how to pay for it, but you need to know they're out there and be able to find and use them easily," notes Lauren Asher, president of TICAS.

Still, with a little digging, students and parents should be able to find most colleges' net price calculators to begin experimenting. *U.S. News* has collated the net price calculators of the top 300 colleges to help launch your investigation.

Chapter 31

10 Things You Need To Know About Net Price Calculators

By KATY HOPKINS

Every college and university in the United States now has its own onlinenet price calculator, a tool that allows prospective students and parents to discover what higher education might actually cost them.

Net price calculators offer a free launching point in the otherwise expensive process of searching for the right college. While campus visit costs and application fees will eventually add up, experimenting with schools' online tools is free to anyone, whether you or your child will be starting college next year or not.

The tools aim to be helpful gadgets for parents and students to add to their college decision arsenals, with the hope of showing what schools with high sticker prices might actually be within a reasonable ballpark for families. Still, they're not made for everyone, and they're not yet fully transparent in what they calculate. Here are some important but often nondescript factors about the tools to keep in mind as you experiment with net price calculators:

1. Who they work for: The federal requirement for net price calculators mandates that schools provide data on first-time, full-time undergraduates. Because school financial aid packages can change dramatically after freshman year, it's important to remember that calculator findings may only be an estimate of your first year of tuition.

2. Who they don't work for: Students who are interested in an out-of-state institution might be out of luck, as public colleges may base calculations on in-state tuition data, financial aid expert Mark Kantrowitz writes in *"Flaws in the Statutory Definition of Net Price."*

The calculators are not applicable to any undergraduate international students, who are increasingly expected to pay full tuition at budget-strapped U.S. universities. (If you are an international student, try contacting the financial aid offices of the colleges you're considering.)

Additionally, unless a school specifically builds in a section for graduate students, anyone interested in pursuing law or medicine, among other advanced degrees, will not be able to estimate their net costs.

3. What years they're good for: The federal requirement did not mandate a specific year of data to use. Therefore, some colleges might currently be basing cost estimates on what freshmen paid in the 2009-2010 school year; others will be using 2010-2011 school year information.

Most importantly, no calculator is currently using data that is applicable to years in the future. This will be especially problematic for parents who hope to get an accurate estimate of the tuition cost for a child who is still very young. Keep in mind that tuition will likely increase beyond what your calculator estimates.

4. What you'll need to use them: To get the most accurate net price calculator estimate possible, you'll need to have a strong grasp of your family's financial situation. For some calculators, you might need to haveincome and tax statements at hand—or a parent close by who knows the numbers. While some calculators take less than 10 minutes to use, it may be best to allot a significant amount of time for experimentation with more in-depth calculators.

Keep your information close by; you'll need to re-enter your data into the calculators of each school you're considering.

5. What they include: Net price is defined as the total cost of school (tuition, room and board, and other expenses) minus the amount of need-based aid you receive based on your family's financial situation. At a minimum, the tools will provide an estimate of need-based aid in your calculations.

Some schools have opted to add other estimates, such as scholarships you might be eligible for, too, though many have not. If merit aid isn't included in the calculation of a school you're interested in, remember that your costs may ultimately be different once scholarships are considered. Be wary of school calculators that also subtract loans from your final estimate; those are costs you will have to pay back one day.

6. What they calculate: Even at schools with the most comprehensive calculators, the findings will be estimates, not the actual figure you'll be paying if you're admitted and enroll. Your true net price could be thousands of dollars more or less than what a calculator estimated, depending on factors such as decreases in school aid, increasing tuition, or a change in your family's financial situation.

7. What they don't produce: Schools are required to include this disclaimer, but make sure you're clear: Calculator findings are in no way a guarantee that you'll be admitted to a certain college or, if you are accepted, that you'll receive a set amount of funding in your first year or in subsequent years.

8. How they might differ: The federal government created a free calculator template for all schools to use. However, many schools have opted for other calculators, either created by a vendor or by the school itself, that might be more accurate to their individual institutions. Because of this and the reasons listed above, the net price estimate you'll receive using one school's calculator may not be comparable to the estimate you get using another institution's tool.

9. Where you might find them: Schools are required to have a calculator—not to have one that's easy to find. While some colleges prominently display their calculators on their financial aid websites, othernet price calculators are much harder to find.

To make it easier for you, *U.S. News* has tracked down net price calculators for more than 250 top colleges.

10. What their limitations mean for you: While you won't get a perfect picture of the price of college, net price calculators, if used correctly, should give you a relatively accurate ballpark figure.

The estimates might show a prospective student that a school with an extremely high sticker price is actually affordable with need-based aid, or might motivate parents of young children to start saving early. Just remember to take each finding with a grain of salt, and not to rule out one school because its calculation is less than another's—for all the reasons above.

If you have any questions as you experiment with net price calculators, contact the financial aid offices of the colleges you are considering.

Chapter 32

How and Why To Get An On-Campus Job

By JULIE MAYFIELD, LINDSEY MAYFIELD

Many students want or need to work during college, but not all jobs are created equal. Working on campus is something every student should give serious consideration.

Julie Mayfield and Lindsey Mayfield highlight the pros and cons of working during college.

JULIE:

Recently, I attended a Parent Association Advisory Board meeting at the University of Kansas, and the conversation turned to students working during college. The college administrators present reminded me of the special advantages of working on campus. Here are a few:

1. A school-friendly schedule: No one understands the demands on a college student quite like campus employers. They're also familiar with the college schedule, including breaks and finals, and tend to work around those if possible.

2. A financial solution: A campus job can sometimes be part of a student's financial package, in the form of a work-study job. Filling out the FAFSA will help your child know if he or she is eligible for this kind of aid.

3. Caring adults: College is a time of transition. Most students aren't children anymore, but they aren't quite adults, either—at least when they first arrive at school. A campus job ensures that your child will regularly come into contact with adults who generally have his or her best interest in mind.

4. Great references: Those caring adults mentioned above can also be the source of some great references for future employment or graduate school. If your student works to secure a job in his or her field of study, those references will be even more valuable.

LINDSEY:

I didn't work during my freshman year of school, but at the beginning of my sophomore year I knew I wanted to get a job, and I wanted it to be on campus. These types of jobs, however, are harder to come by than you might think. Here's a few ways to make your campus job search more successful:

1. Cast a wide net: While I had always wanted to work in the library or the journalism school, those weren't the jobs for which I got interviews.

135

I applied for 10 campus jobs at the beginning of the year, got interviews for three, and only one ended up working out for me. If you're really interested in a campus job, don't be too picky about which one it is; most of them are relatively similar.

2. Follow up: Supervisors for campus jobs differ from supervisors at other jobs, because they often double as lecturers, researchers, authors, and more.

Hiring a student assistant is not always at the top of their to-do lists, so keeping in touch with them may be what sets you apart from the rest of the applicants.

3. Be professional: It may sound like common sense to be professional in a job interview, but I have seen too many of my peers go to interviews underdressed or acting too informal.

A campus job interview is still an interview, so treat it like one. Shake the person's hand, show up five minutes early, and never wear jeans. These are some of the easiest ways to show the employer that you are serious about the position.

Chapter 33

5 Financial Surprises for College Parents

By KATY HOPKINS

During high school, many students and parents likely learn the basics of paying for college, from tuition costs to scholarship possibilities. But when it's time to actually pay the bills, even well-prepared parents may face some financial surprises.

Here are a few of the biggest shocks parents say they had as they began to pay for college.

1. Textbooks: The Tirloni family anticipated spending money on science textbooks for their daughter, a freshman studying biology at Texas A&M University. But they were still taken aback when the first semester's textbook bill totaled about $1,000, mother Kristina says.

"I had no idea the price of books had gone up so high," says Tirloni, who lives in Texas. "The price of books was the most startling up-front cost we had."

Next semester, she says, the family will consider used options on Amazon before opting for a prepackaged bundle of new books at the campus bookstore.

2. Parent expenses: Parents aren't enrolling in college, but they could still have expenses associated with the college experience. North Carolina resident Julie Rains wanted to take part in her son's orientation at the University of North Carolina—Chapel Hill, but between the fees for the parent sessions and a hotel room near campus that allowed her to make the early morning meetings, the event added up to a sizable, and unexpected, college cost.

"You're starting to run $400 to $500—I think my parents paid that for a semester when I was in school," says Rains, a UNC alumnus, of the parent orientation. "The orientation session was very valuable as a parent; it was just an extra cost."

3. Meal plans: Food is an unavoidable cost for any student, but the campus meal plan could result in wasted money if funds are left over after the first term. Some universities allow students to scale back their plans mid-semester, or to roll excess points or dollars over to the spring semester. For the Tirloni family, though, extra meal points are hurriedly being spent on bulk items like cases of water at the on-campus convenience store.

"[My daughter] has a ton of money left in her account," Tirloni says. "That's money you paid for, and you lose it. Going forward, we're really going to be more cognizant of what she's spending."

4. Student loan interest rates: Student loans are often included incollege financial aid award packages. But loans aren't free money—they need to be paid back, with added interest.

With two sons in college, the Schaffer family was shocked by their financing options, mother Judy says. The family ultimately used a home equity line of credit (HELOC) to help fund degrees at Touro College and Johns Hopkins University, after they didn't qualify for substantial work-study funds and shied away from interest rates on private student loans, she says.

"We expected [work-study] to be higher; we expected interest rates to be lower," says Schaffer, whose family is from New Jersey. "To ask him to get loans at 6, 7, 8 percent when we can get a loan at 3 is not financially smart."

If you have questions about student loan interest rates and funding options, reach out to college financial aid administrators, who should be able to help you evaluate choices based on your family's situation.

5. Scholarships: There are many opportunities for college scholarships, but finding the funding might take some digging. "I think people put a lot of responsibility on high school and college

advisers, and even colleges themselves, in finding [scholarship] programs for their students," Schaffer says. "It's really on the students' and parents' shoulders to find this stuff."

Learning from experience, the Rains family's second son will start his scholarship search earlier in high school, Rains says, and will cater each application essay to the colleges he applies to, in hopes of standing out for additional funding.

"If we had paid more attention to the application process, not just in terms of seeing it as an application for entrance but seeing it as a key to getting scholarships, that would have been more helpful," Rains says.

Chapter 34

How To Start Paying Off Student Loans

By KATY HOPKINS

During college, students who need to take loans may not give much thought to the accumulating financial burden. With no bills coming for months after graduation, preparing for repayment may not take immediate priority.

"They're thinking about graduating and looking for a job, and have kind of put off the idea of what they're going to owe until they leave," says Chris George, assistant vice chancellor for enrollment and director of financial aid at the University of Denver.

But the six-month grace period some loans offer is likely over for class of 2012 graduates—meaning it's time to kick off a repayment plan now. Here's how to get started.

1. Face your debt: If your loans have been building, a crucial first step is to know what you're working with. On the National Student Loan Data System, students can locate all their federal loans and find debt totals, including accumulated interest.

"Before I looked online, I wasn't even sure how much my loans were, including interest," says Meghan Mitnick, a teacher in New York City with six-figure loan debt from two New York University degrees. "Even though it's really scary, know exactly what you're dealing with."

2. Contact your loan servicer: Once you know how much you owe, find out exactly who you'll be sending checks to—your student loan servicer.

"That's the question we get often: Who am I supposed to be paying?" says George of the University of Denver.

Whether you have federal or private loans, your loan servicer is your first point of contact for any questions and address updates, so don't hesitate to reach out, recommends Erin Wolfe, associate director of financial aid at Susquehanna University.

"The best advice for any graduate is to remain proactive in loan repayment," Wolfe wrote in an E-mail. "If you have questions or concerns, contact the loan servicer without delay. Building a successful repayment strategy for student loan debt is essential for shaping the borrower's financial future."

3. Pick a repayment plan: The standard repayment plan for student loans is 10 years, but that doesn't necessarily make it the right option for every student.

Some borrowers of federal student loans, for example, may be better off opting into Income-Based Repayment or Income-Contingent Repaymentplans, which adjust monthly bills according to pay. For help finding the right plan, online tools such as PayBackSmarter.com allow students to experiment with payment options.

4. Stick to a budget: Once you determine a monthly obligation, keep track of other spending to ensure you can pay all your bills. Websites such as Mint.com help University of Pittsburgh graduate Shawn Norcross as he prepares to begin repaying about $83,000 worth of student loans, he says.

"Budgeting is amazing, because whenever you can actually see it on a website or on your phone, you don't want to go over; you don't want to cheat," says Norcross, who compares financial tracking to counting calories. "It almost turns into a game of sorts where you want to win."

5. Prioritize your loan payments: As you budget, you may find yourself forgoing activities or events to pay off your debt. For Pitt graduate Norcross, his upcoming payments have already taken precedence over major decisions as he plans to avoid default, he says.

"My student loans are affecting my life. The plan was for me and my girlfriend to move to D.C. by now, but I just can't do it—

it's not financially feasible for me," Norcross says. "My student loan payments are probably No. 1."

Prioritizing may also mean minimizing other forms of debt or, if possible, chipping away at student loans before tackling other types of debt.

"Student loans are one of the few debt obligations that are rarely forgiven in bankruptcy filings," notes Michael Scott, director of scholarships and student financial aid at Texas Christian University. "In a worst case scenario, you will be better off if you've reduced non-dischargeable debt first."

6. Focus on the future: If you find you're scrimping or sacrificing to make your monthly student loan payments, it may help to remind yourself what you're paying for.

"I really value the education I got, and I got a good job, so it paid off," NYU graduate Mitnick says. "Right now it seems like a lot, but in 10 or 15 years ... it will be worth it."

Contributor Bios

Robert Berger

Rob Berger is the founder of the popular personal finance blog, the Dough Roller. He is also the editor of the Dough Roller Newsletter, a free weekly newsletter with tips and resources to help readers improve their finances.

Kim Clark

Kim Clark is a veteran journalist with more than 20 years of experience, specializes in college financial aid, personal finance, business, and economics.

Reyna Gobel

Reyna Gobel is a freelance education reporter for U.S. News, covering college savings. You can follow her on Twitter or email her at reyna@graduationdebt.org.

Katy Hopkins

Katy Hopkins is an education reporter for U.S. News

Neda Jafarzadeh

Neda Jafarzadeh is a financial analyst at NerdWallet Investing, a financial literacy organization that helps investors select better mutual funds, figure out where to open IRA accounts and make smarter investment decisions overall.

Julie and Lindsey Mayfield

Julie and Lindsey Mayfield are a mother-daughter duo tackling the college experience for the first time. Julie is a finance blogger at The Family CEO and the mother of two: a son in high school who is weighing his college options, and a daughter, Lindsey, who is a junior studying journalism and political science at the University of Kansas. Got a question? E-mail them attwicetheadvice@usnews.com or follow Julie on Facebook and Twitter.

Eugene L. Meyer

Eugene L. Meyer is a contributor at U.S. News.

Kelsey Sheehy

Kelsey Sheehy is an education reporter at U.S. News, covering high schools and college financing. You can follow her on Twitter or email her at ksheehy@usnews.com

Justin Snider

Justin Snider is an advising dean at Columbia University, where he also teaches undergraduate writing. This article was produced by The Hechinger Report, a nonprofit, nonpartisan education news outlet affiliated with the Hechinger Institute on Education and the Media, based at Columbia's Teachers College.

Scholarship America

Scholarship America® is a national organization that helps students get into and graduate from college through three core programs: Dollars for Scholars®, DreamkeepersSM® and Scholarship Management Services®. More than $2.7 billion in scholarships and education assistance has been awarded to more than 1.8 million students since 1958. Their scholarship administration expertise has helped nearly 1,100 communities and more than 1,100 corporations develop and implement local scholarship programs.

CPSIA information can be obtained at www.ICGtesting.com
Printed in the USA
LVOW05s2154301014

411364LV00013B/207/P